HOODED

HOODED

A Black Girl's Guide to the Ph.D.

DR. MALIKA GRAYSON

Books may be purchased in quantity and/or special sales by contacting the publisher.

Mynd Matters Publishing
715 Peachtree Street NE
Suites 100 & 200
Atlanta, GA 30308
www.myndmatterspublishing.com

Cover design by Lo Harris

978-1-953307-02-6 (pbk)
978-1-953307-03-3 (ebook)

FIRST EDITION

*For every Black Woman on her
journey towards higher education.
I am your tribe.*

CONTENTS

A MILE IN OUR SHOES

Have you ever felt out of place? Have you questioned whether your opinions or contributions would be rejected simply because of your race? That's what it's like to be a Black woman in graduate school.

Just the thought of being a graduate student can weigh heavily on anyone's psyche. Not only must you think differently from how you did as an undergraduate student; you are also expected to work independently for the first time. Now, imagine the added stress of being a woman in the male-dominated fields of STEM (science, technology, engineering, and mathematics). Imagine being a Black woman. Two for two, if you ask me.

Pulling the race card is a quick way to make a few readers uncomfortable, but this topic—and the bias it presents—is embedded in our society. A look at our current political climate is a clear indicator of this. Whether we encounter discrimination in the classroom or the workforce, it is our job to dismantle it, as so many have done before us.

When I began to visit varying STEM graduate programs across the country, I immediately noticed a recurring trend: the lack of Black people. At each stop, I thought, "Where are the people who look like me? Where are all the beautiful, brilliant Black men and women who are going to change the future? Did I miss *our* day?"

I knew that various fields in STEM struggled with diversity, but this seemed ridiculous. Trying my best to not be deterred, I eventually chose to pursue a path in mechanical engineering. Though my choice came rather easily, I was quite oblivious to the struggles that awaited me at the PWI (predominantly white institution) I had chosen to attend. While I knew I would be one of the few minority students in my PhD program, I had no idea that I would also be the only Black woman—a statistic that would remain unchanged for the duration of my program.

Being a person of color pursuing higher education isn't easy. While you battle the constant fear of being discriminated against, you also have to fight through the plague of questions regarding your presence and whether it was rightfully earned. You become entangled within a web of choosing to stand up for yourself and risk being labelled the "angry Black woman," or ignore them and succumb to "respectability." Whichever lane you choose to occupy, there will never be a right way to immediately heal the wounds these assumptions create.

I often naively believe that our accolades should be able to speak for themselves. In the real world, our qualifications will continue to be questioned, no matter how hard we work. Why? Simply because we don't look the part.

In these times of tribulation, I have to acknowledge the blessing it was—and still is—to have strong Black women to lean on. It is also a blessing to have those who don't look like me stand in my corner as allies. The key here is *trust*. I discovered early on that if you are unable to find people you can trust (no matter their ethnicity), the road will be incredibly hard. Choose wisely. I was able to align myself with people who wanted the absolute best for me, but I also met people who only wanted to dim my light in order to brighten their own.

While graduate school will challenge you in ways you never expected, what you gain in the end is truly invaluable. At times, your confidence may be rocked by patronizing and unwarranted comments. Once you regain your footing, it is up to you to decide if you are defined by their assumptions, or if you are going to go beyond their expectations and leave a legacy for every Black woman who comes through those doors.

You may not be able to answer that right now, but I implore you to not give up. That is not what we do. Dr. Rebecca Lee Crumpler didn't; nor did Dr. Sadie Tanner Mossell Alexander. As you embark on this journey, find comfort in knowing that you are in the company of extraordinary women. Be confident knowing that you can overcome any obstacle placed before you—and that you, too, will continue to pave the way for strong, resilient Black women.

Signed,

An Unapologetic Black Woman with a PhD

PROLOGUE

As academics, one of our greatest feats is overcoming each scholarly obstacle placed before us. Our goal, in part, is to graduate knowing that we achieved the one thing to which we've dedicated so much of our lives. It's not lost on us that great sacrifice is required to stay our course. But as we ride the academic wave of uncertainty, we pray to simply make it to the end.

My academic journey to gaining my PhD was no different. After what felt like the most challenging five years of my life, I was finally center stage on graduation day. Mounting the stage that day to receive my doctorate degree was an experience incomparable to any other, and if I'm being quite honest, at some points, I was unsure I'd make it here to see it through to fruition. As I stood there, basking in my crowning moment, I looked out into the sea of fellow graduates and grappled with reality. There were so many faces all starkly different from my own.

In that moment, I was again face-to-face with the unpleasant and familiar feeling that had accompanied me every single step of this trying, momentous journey.

From the day I first arrived at that prestigious PWI, there was one word that haunted me in my many moments of silence: *community*. As I stood there, realizing just how much of my journey had been shaped by the lack of diversity, I decided to tell my story.

But how do you write a story that has been told a thousand times? Or has it? I began writing this memoir and hoped it could be a guide for those who may venture down a lonely, yet familiar, path. I believe that my experiences in STEM as a Black woman have mirrored the thoughts and emotions of others in academia at one point or another. These were often thoughts that vacillated between the fear of failure to the pressure of maintaining success as I maneuvered through each year.

While I tried my absolute best to remain optimistic, graduate school was an emotional journey. At times, I found myself attempting to win a daunting battle between academic and personal strife. This battle brought struggles with depression and immense loss, which unearthed some of my darkest moments.

This may sound perilous, but these moments not only shaped the woman before you, but taught me the power of prayer, self-confidence, and, most importantly, community.

I hope my journey can serve as a guide to finding comfort and community in the tumultuous world of graduate school.

YEAR ONE

"Science is not a boy's game; it's not a girl's game. It's everyone's game."
—Nichelle Nichols

THE JOURNEY

As I swerved back onto the shoulder of the I-81 highway, a car sped by. "This is crazy," I said out loud to myself as I tried to maintain control of my car. It was my first time driving on a highway in the United States, and I somehow thought it would also be a good time to think about everything that was possibly waiting for me in graduate school. But since merging was something I had only read about, I was about to get bullied off the road by passing cars before the journey had even begun.

Isadora, or "Izzy," as I liked to call her, was the name I had given to my Jeep Cherokee in memory of my late grandmother. My mother complained about me naming my car after her, but since I never met my grandmother, the simple gesture felt special to me. I didn't know it at the time, but this car was going to be more than just a mode of transportation. It would be the vehicle that would accompany me through my first strides into a new world of independence and constant assimilation.

Making the five-hour drive from Brooklyn, New York, to a small town in upstate New York proved to be more than just the 200-mile stretch of highway. In a way, it symbolized the lengthy journey ahead of me and the multiple times I would find myself almost swerving completely off the road before being able to gather my bearings. If I didn't get back on track as quickly as possible, it could end up costing me dearly.

After finishing high school in the beautiful Republic of Trinidad and Tobago (where I was raised), I was excited to venture out into the world and explore where my interests in applied sciences could take me. At first, it took me to New York City, where I would complete my undergraduate studies. There, I met some of my closest friends, who I still cherish to this very day.

However, as I neared the end of my undergraduate journey, graduating was my sole focus. The very concept of life beyond graduation was a blur, and something I truly didn't have the bandwidth to delve deeper into. Between balancing a full plate that overflowed with a demanding course load, work-study duties, and student organization commitments, who could? I'm sure that we can all agree that when our wants change so often, it can be too stressful to think too far in the future. The avoidance especially peaks when every person you encounter during your senior year asks the same question: "So, what are you doing after graduation?"

I really hadn't considered graduate school until I attended a summer undergraduate research experience. The experience was everything I didn't know I needed, yet it somehow altered the scope of what I thought was possible. Prior to that, my only thought about graduate school was the exorbitant debt students incur, and I was already thinking about how I was going to repay my hefty undergraduate loans. No one tells you that, regardless of your situation, your loan payments are due six months after graduation. Initially, the sheer joy of being in college sucks you in, and you find yourself accepting every form of financial aid that is offered. But towards the end, when the final loan repayment amount is revealed, financial "aid" starts to weigh heavily on your every thought. The idea of willingly signing up for more debt seemed ludicrous.

Thanks to my summer research mentor, my thoughts about graduate school began to shift. Learning that graduate school could somehow rid me of my current and future debts made the decision less stressful. Despite this alleviated burden, I first had to answer the most important question: was graduate school for me?

The summer experience had opened me up to the

field of engineering and had given me a deeper understanding of how being an applied science major related to the world around me. I saw engineering as a way to take me from applied science to somewhere far beyond what I had imagined. In that moment, graduate school became an opportunity to explore new dreams.

As I continued my drive, the rows of empty fields hugged each side of the highway and swallowed me in its vastness. In this moment, it was me against the world. Filled with nothing but endless possibilities, this was my new beginning.

By the time I arrived in my new town, it felt as if the entire day had raced past me. With only a few suitcases of clothing and boxes of textbooks I had acquired during my time in undergrad, I was grateful for the one-story climb to my new apartment. The only person I met that night was the property manager, who gave me my keys. As the apartment door quietly closed behind me, reality began to sink in. It was just me. The closest familiar face was now over 250 miles away.

As night approached, I sat on my blow-up mattress and stared at the white-washed walls of my apartment. I began to imagine them as my canvas. I tried to paint a picture of what the next five years of my life would look like, but the complexity of my emotions began to make the room grow increasingly smaller. Eventually, it became easier to be consumed by the deafening silence of upstate New York. Through exhausted tears, I thought of everything I had left behind, and forced myself to sleep. Tomorrow was going to be a long day of exploring.

Upstate New York is a vast contrast from New York City. If you've never been to New York City, the first things that probably come to mind are landmarks like Times Square or the Statue of Liberty. Some may even envision crowded subway trains, hordes of taxi cabs, and swarms of abrasive people all fighting for their place in the concrete jungle. My new environment in upstate New York was a beautiful anomaly. Here, I would be able to see the stars at night and inhale nature in its truest form. Though I lived on campus throughout my undergraduate years, I was now forced to assimilate to the culture of a new, even smaller community. The town had the essentials: a supermarket everyone obsessed over, the staple Walmart and Target, and dozens of local restaurants and businesses.

On my first day, also known as the first day of the

rest of my twenties, everyone else just seemed to *belong*. It was as if they had been preparing for this moment their entire lives. Meanwhile, here I was, looking around wondering if anyone else felt as uncomfortable or out of place as I did. As I wondered, I scrutinized myself, and was confident that others were scrutinizing me as well. Being the only Black person in a sea of so many white bodies left me with the notion that I needed to do more than just do well—I needed to excel. The heaviness of feeling as though I had to singlehandedly dismantle the many preconceived ideas about minorities in academia— especially Black women—began to curl my shoulders. I had to prove that they were both wrong and undeserved.

To be honest, it was about more than just filling a "quota." In the back of my mind, I knew that I belonged there. I had worked tirelessly for three years, studying nothing but physics during my undergraduate studies. Before that, I was a child with various curiosities about the world of science and questioned how everything worked. I knew my spot was earned by the grocery list of accomplishments, but in this new environment, it would take a little more self-convincing.

My first order of business was to attend a seminar with the rest of my cohort. As I looked around the room, I couldn't find a familiar skin tone. It soon became clear that I was the only Black person in my year. This brought on feelings of intense pressure, as I no longer felt as though my presence was simply about me, my research, or my future graduation.

There was also the pressure of knowing that I was representing every other Black woman who had ever started a PhD program, but was unable to finish due to life's uncertainties. This was also for every Black woman who had ever had someone question her worth or capabilities.

Occasionally, opportunities come our way that are meant to define who we are and who we become. For me, this was one of those opportunities. Whether I was ready or not, the challenge had begun.

THE PROGRAM

I remember my first class so vividly, and yet, the content of what was taught that day remains a blur. I had gone from being one of the top students in my undergraduate department to being someone who wished to be invisible every time they stepped into a classroom. Equations and definitions seemed to haunt me as they flew over my head, and I silently begged for mercy. I wondered how I was going to be the change I wished to see in the world when every assignment made it feel like I was falling off a cliff. This may sound dramatic, but bear with me as I try to convey my experience.

After completing my undergraduate degree in physics, mechanical engineering was a whole new world. I was accustomed to the theory of how things worked—not the practicality engineering required. The shared dependency on professors and advisors was vastly different from the independence of graduate school, where no one was bothered if I chose to attend classes. I was now in complete control of what classes I needed to take, and the strategic placement of each. Whatever classes I took needed to fit in perfectly with the other puzzle pieces of my PhD. It was almost as though I was forced to unlearn everything I thought I knew and restructure the way my mind had been trained to retain information.

Compared to the way I maneuvered through academia before this point, it all seemed calculated—and to be honest, it was overwhelming. I always prided myself as being an exemplary student, but it was beginning to look like that title was up for grabs.

For as long as I can remember, my parents reminded me that, as one of the few Afro-Caribbean students, I would always have to work twice as hard as my counterparts. By simply being Black in these spaces, I was already at a disadvantage; this was no different in college. As a Black woman in the undergraduate physics department, I had even more to prove. To get by, I made an art of checking off all the boxes that ensured nothing could get in my way or slow the trajectory I had mapped out for myself. But my new reality—the learning, research, and expectations of it all—left me completely defeated.

It is important to note that at the end of five years, the cost of a PhD student to their school and dissertation advisor is roughly $250,000. This usually includes tuition, stipends, and if you're lucky, health insurance. Considering those costs, I couldn't help but question if my presence was really worth it. Was I worth up to a quarter of a million dollars? If I had been forced to answer this question honestly at the time, I would have said no. Thankfully, the decision wasn't up to me.

After the first few months of endless stress and confusion, time seemed to pick up out of nowhere. Before I knew it, October had arrived. This was the point in my first year where I was expected to choose a professor who would serve as my dissertation advisor. As you will come to learn, this is a crucial decision that comes early on in your graduate school journey. Your dissertation advisor is the person who will guide you through your research. Their role is to offer constructive guidance and provide unmitigated access to resources, such as lab equipment, grant money, and collaborators. In a nutshell, their purpose is to ensure you have everything you need to be successful. The advisor you choose will also go on to be the head of your dissertation committee, which will most likely comprise of other professors who are familiar with your field of choice.

They will also help you gauge how you can best advance your field. But don't worry; you usually don't have to choose a dissertation committee until you have confirmed your research topic of choice.

As I searched for an advisor, I knew I needed them to be someone I could depend on from topic conception to completion and everything in between. I needed someone who would work to maintain a place for me in my program, in the unfortunate event that I was unable to attain a fellowship. A fellowship is money awarded to doctoral students that subsidizes the costs related to graduate school including tuition and cost-of-living stipend, though it varies depending on the discipline. Without the burden of securing their own funding, a doctoral student can then work on his or her research without working outside of the department or school. All things considered, I needed my future advisor to be not only an advocate, but the sponsor and mentor I so desperately needed.

Despite meeting with numerous potential dissertation advisors, none of them seemed to be the right fit. I wanted someone I could connect with on an academic and personal level, who would also understand the challenges I may experience as a woman of color in a predominantly white, male space. Truthfully, the department lacked not only people of color, but women as well.

The possibility of relying on a someone who didn't look like me to be my ally left me ridden with anxiety. Of course, I chose this school for the program and research opportunities, but before that moment, I didn't realize how much the lack of representation would affect me and the decisions I made. In addition to the lack of familiarity I felt with each advisor, I was also unable to find someone whose research piqued my interest enough to take it to the next step. This was actually ironic, since I had no idea what my interests were.

After a few weeks, I began to wonder if my sales pitch needed some work. I felt partially to blame, because I was so indecisive about what I wanted my future in graduate school to look like. If I couldn't see what the next five years had in store for me, how could they? In any event, I remained optimistic that I would eventually find my perfect match.

After an extensive search, my potential advisor list was down to two professors—both men of color. I was having frequent meetings with both of them. I was leaning towards one, because I discovered we shared a similar Caribbean upbringing. But to my disappointment, his lab was already packed with students. There was still room for me, but I questioned if I would be able to get the undivided mentorship and attention I needed. Not known to be the most outspoken person, I didn't want to compete for a professor's already limited time and eventually fall through the cracks.

Though both professors were brilliant, I was still trying to figure out what I wanted from them, and most importantly, from myself. I had spent so much of my life wanting to find a way to use my hands and apply it to the world of science that I was unsure which field of engineering would fit me best. I knew I needed someone who would support me in figuring it out, and I hoped they would also be open to innovative ideas to help me push the envelope.

After I had narrowed my search, I was hesitant to break the news to the professors I chose not to work with. I was afraid of burning bridges. With no Black professors in my department, I needed all the allies I could get. It was important that I showed my gratitude for their time and expressed my respect for their research. I also needed to clarify that this simply meant another lab was better suited to accommodate my needs and future aspirations. As silly as it may seem, the decision was beginning to weigh heavily on me.

Then one day, it magically clicked. During one of my many meetings with the professor who shared a similar Caribbean background, he said, "Stick with me, and I will make sure you find something that you are passionate about." His words were so simple and matter-of-fact, but from that moment on, I no longer had any doubts about who my advisor would be. His confidence had assured me that I was making the right decision, and I felt safe under his guidance. I believed that I could be honest with him about my fears, and they wouldn't be used against me. His always calm and composed candor would be something I'd grow to rely on, especially in times of severe self-doubt. Making this decision felt like a burden had been lifted, but before I could get too comfortable, graduate school had much more in store.

THE WHY

By the second semester of my first year, I was beyond overwhelmed, and that was just from my required classes. I had yet to begin brainstorming ideas for my research problem or read any of the necessary literature reviews that would help me choose. I was barely making it through my class assignments each night, and was often greeted by the sunrise in the computer lab the following morning.

While I fought to barely keep my head above water, the end of the semester was quickly approaching. I only had mere weeks before I was scheduled to take my qualifying exam, which was a prerequisite to assess my qualifications and readiness for the PhD program. This exam would determine if my foundation was solid enough for me to become an official PhD student.

I had to be honest with myself and admit just how poorly I was performing. Based on how long it took me to complete my assignments, I knew that I was in no shape to stand in front of a qualification exam panel while they grilled me on what I knew. I mean, let's face it—I was not an engineer! At least, not yet.

The transition from physics to engineering was already more difficult than anticipated. I only had one summer of research experience under my belt and knew that I needed more time. All my hardships were strong indicators that I needed to delay the exam. However, I was worried my advisor would see my request for postponement as a sign of incompetence— the one thing I was hoping to avoid.

As my exam day drew closer, my nerve disappeared into the shadows. I felt completely exposed each time I thought of my pending request. Would this be the thing to kick me off track before I had even gotten started? Not only did I have to go through my advisor, I also had to be granted a six-month allowance by the department chair. Rather than take the exam in June, I was going to request to take it the following January over the winter break. With everything riding on this exam, I would also be spending Christmas away from my family for the first time—the first of many sacrifices to come.

The morning of my meeting, I looked at myself in the mirror and could see nothing but disappointment. I felt as though I had taken a spot from a more brilliant and deserving Black woman who would have been better equipped for this fight. I know it seems harsh, but I believed I needed to be my own worst critic. I knew if I was satisfied with myself, then I would excel in everything else. I had set the bar so high.

As I walked into the chair's office, I wondered what his reaction would be. When my time came, I reluctantly explained my situation as honestly as I could. I expressed that, despite my hardest efforts, the transition from physics to mechanical engineering had been much harder than I thought. Though I tried my absolute hardest to adjust to the new learning curve, I had also grossly underestimated the toll it would have on me. I showed him the letter I had received from my advisor in support of the extension I was requesting. My advisor also agreed that an extra six months of preparation time and additional summer classes would be best.

While I poured my heart out, he was emotionless, offering no sign that he empathized or even understood my struggle. Finally, he asked, "What if you decide that six months from now, you're still not ready? Are you sure this is what you want?"

I replied meekly, "I will be ready."

I had tried my best to hide the fact that all confidence was slowly escaping from my body, but waves of self-doubt immediately flooded the room. Maybe he was right. What if after six months I was still at square one? I wouldn't be able to come back from that type of embarrassment.

I took a moment to weigh my options. I could always return home and tell my friends and family that after much deliberation, I had elected to drop out of the engineering program. Perhaps engineering wasn't the right fit for me after all, and a career in physics would prove to be the more practical choice. Then I remembered why I had decided to embark on this journey in the first place. I hated to admit it, but I had lost sight of why I had chosen this program. I chose it because of my advisor, the new people I'd meet, and the experiences I'd endure. But mostly, I chose it for the new life I could create for myself in STEM.

I had spent the entire year trying so hard to convince my classmates (unbeknownst to them) that I had "earned" my spot. Once reality set in, I had to remind myself that nothing I did was for their acceptance or approval. I was here for me, and for others who looked like me. Their acceptance wasn't necessary, nor was it needed. I wanted to learn more to expand my knowledge base, which was going to be difficult. Engineering was its own language filled with unfamiliar jargon; I knew I was finally ready to become bilingual.

I spent the summer sitting in on every available class I could find. I audited classes. Auditing a class is much harder than actually taking a class for credit. Admittedly, this is a good lesson in discipline and commitment. To get the most out of each lecture, you also have to do the work that comes along with it. To ensure my time wasn't in vain, professors agreed to grade the work I submitted—even though I wasn't enrolled. The goal was to note my progress, and the sacrifice seemed to be paying off.

Like any vacation, the summer flew by before I had ever gotten a chance to enjoy it. Before long, I was once again back in my enrolled classes. This time, however, the velocity of my spinning head was reduced to a slow whirl. I felt more open to new information, but for some reason, the connection with the subject matter was still missing. It took me twice as long as other students to understand the notes that were given. You may wonder why I didn't ask more questions. Well, it took me just as long to write and read notes in class; I wasn't able to even formulate a question to ask. By the time I truly got it, the topic had changed, or we were already at the end of the lecture. There were several times when I realized that some of the points had simply gone over my head.

My frustrations grew as this became a recurring incident in every class and larger lab meetings. I came to my breaking point and decided to see the school nurse. It was becoming increasingly clear that I needed to talk to someone, and I was starting to worry because my mind always seemed to be one step behind everyone else's. After our first meeting, she recommended that I meet with a psychologist. I booked the next available appointment.

Initially, I was skeptical and wondered if this was yet another sign of weakness. But for once, I didn't hold back. I let out all my frustrations: my anger, my tears, my doubts, and my fears. I told myself that the worst that could happen was that I would never see her again. Maybe it would serve as a one-time confessional.

Instead of closing the file after our initial session, he asked about my availability for the following weeks. He thought it would be a good idea to perform a series of tests to help me determine my strengths and weaknesses, and I agreed. Once the tests were over, I was diagnosed with CAPD—better known as central auditory processing disorder. This meant that while I could hear information being relayed to me perfectly, the way I processed it was different from others. Basically, it takes me twice as long for things "to stick," especially when the information was relayed orally. Rather than feeling relieved, I was angry with myself. Once again, everyone else had a head start. I was so focused on proving myself to my peers that I had completely neglected myself and my needs. What was the point of being the strong, brilliant Black woman if I was going to push myself to my breaking point in the process?

I wondered if I had the same symptoms in undergraduate school, but never took the time to pay attention to them. Back then, I was studying around the clock to keep up with lectures and pass my classes. I would cram, read, and re-read until I remembered the material. If I had taken the time to visit someone then, would everything be easier?

I had to ask myself if I would let this prevent me from becoming an expert in my field. The truth is that I thought about using this as an excuse (once again) to not continue with my program. It would have been an easy way out, and many would have understood my reason for giving up. As I thought about the immediate future—the qualifying exam, and the research that would follow—things began to feel even more intimidating. Why put myself through the exam, knowing how difficult it would be? In my mind, it seemed better to simply commit to one more year, earn a master's degree, and be done with it. If I chose to continue to a PhD, it would be a steep battle to the end. No, thanks!

At this point, my plans for moving forward were getting dimmer. I had already made my decision. I wouldn't put myself through the exam. I would still get a degree—just not the one I initially enrolled for.

YEAR ONE LESSONS

THE ACCLIMATION

We have all heard that it takes time to acclimate to a new environment. Until you get into the swing of things, you can't fully immerse yourself in the graduate experience. The question is, do Black women really acclimate to graduate school? After all, "to acclimate" is defined as "becoming accustomed to a new climate or new conditions." Do we really get accustomed? How can we? After all, we must be comfortable in the environment we're in before we can begin to be ourselves. But how do we, as Black female graduate students, do that? We don't.

We process, and then we TRANSFORM.

To make it through, we seek out strength that we never even knew we possessed. We become passionate about our future and become suddenly aware of the individuals who we believe can impact it. We become self-motivators who are fully cognizant of our surroundings and the people who are vastly different from us, and as such, we thrive for perfection. So, how do we transform in this new environment?

THE LOCATION

Location, location, location. Remember, you must be ready and willing to commit to a place as much as you are willing to commit to a school. I gave very little thought to the town I would be living in when I chose this school. In hindsight, I should have. Simple things such as airport accessibility and flight cancellations due to inclement weather were common issues. They may seem like things that can be overlooked, but when you combine those with all the other "simple" setbacks, each one adds a layer of frustration to your overall experience. Though I got accustomed to small-town living quite quickly, and found that it relaxed me in many ways, I also had friends who ended up being miserable in the same situation. Are you a rural girl, or an urban girl? Does it even matter? Your surroundings can affect your mood, so it's important to consider how isolation can impact your thoughts and your overall mental health.

THE WORK/LIFE ADJUSTMENT

The transition in course requirements is difficult and requires you be more self-sufficient and resourceful than you were before. Allow your classmates to become your homework buddies and utilize the availabilities of your TAs (teaching assistants). Always remember that even though you may think someone has all the answers, everyone is faking it—they may benefit from the "stupid" questions you are too afraid to ask. Remember, professors need to go at a speed that benefits your learning capacity. If you aren't sure, ask.

As you start your journey, remember one thing: by simply being in these rooms, we are advocates. We are accomplishing what we hope others will someday accomplish without the hardships we endured. Don't just assimilate—TRANSFORM.

The first year is filled with so much coursework that it may feel overwhelming at times. If nothing else, remember to:

STUDY F.A.S.T.

Focus on the key points and tasks.

Alternate your surroundings. Your location either helps or hinders your learning and progress.

Surround yourself with people who will not only be helpful, but also uplift you and your spirits.

Timing is everything. Take the necessary time for your mind and body to rest. Remember that the entire process is an adjustment, so take it in stride.

END OF CHAPTER WORKSHOP

Doing What's RIGHT: Research Topic

How did I go about choosing the right research topic? Here, the word "right" means "right for you."

How did I know it was right for me? I was able to combine something that felt familiar with something innovative. Although I didn't finalize my research question till the end of year two, I wish I had started at least the exploration process sooner.

To explore things further, answer these key questions:
- What am I passionate about?
- What topics do I enjoy learning about?
- Can I study this topic for an extended number of years, and will I have the patience for it even on the days I am tired of it?
- Is my topic going to add to my chosen field?

Doing What's RIGHT: Advisor

How did I go about choosing the **right** advisor? Here, the word "right" means "right for you."

I mentioned earlier in the chapter that I needed my future advisor to be an advocate, sponsor, and mentor—and that it took me a few interviews to make that choice. Here are a few questions I asked myself when looking for the person who would be a great fit:

- What is their background, and how does it compliment mine and my goals?
- Does this individual have the time and bandwidth to be invested in me?
- What makes them an effective advisor (are they respected?), and what is the feedback from other students?
- Does this person have the qualities and characteristics I look for and admire in a mentor?
- Will I be able to gain knowledge, professional growth, and opportunities under this person's tutelage?
- As a non-Black person, will this individual understand any challenges I will encounter because of my skin color?

- What relationship do they have with the diversity office or point of contacts at the school?

These questions don't require answers right away; however, if you are new to graduate school, they should be considered (especially as you network with potential advisors).

YEAR TWO

"Courage is like—it's a habitus, a habit, a virtue; you get it by courageous acts. It's like you learn to swim by swimming. You learn courage by encouraging."
—Marie M. Daly

THE DECISION

During the toughest challenges, I would always reminisce on being back home in Trinidad. Until the age of thirteen, I was sure that I was destined to become a doctor. My aunt was one of the top nurses in Trinidad and Tobago, and for much of her career, she lent her talents to communities in need. I always admired the way she was able to immediately diagnose my aches and pains. I thought to myself, *I want to be just like that: a fixer of people*. But, to my chagrin, biology had other plans for me, and I knew that having an MD behind my name was not in the cards.

Instead, I found something else that better suited my skills and left me feeling impassioned. I was better at fixing things with my hands. In my free time, I was known to spend hours taking things apart and putting them back together. I always enjoyed being able to analyze a problem and find its solution. Later, I was tasked with solving the puzzle of how I could piece together all the things I loved to form a cohesive career. I had a glimpse of what that could look like, but I had no clue what it was even called.

I grew up exposed to teachers, coaches, and librarians, all dedicated to the educational system. As

I left the shores of my Caribbean twin isles, the conversation surrounding STEM felt foreign to me— but it also piqued my interest. It was a buzz term I didn't hear until college, and I had no idea how one complemented the other. Though I was exposed to physics, chemistry, and biology in their respective worlds, I had yet to be exposed to engineering in any capacity.

As I did some more research, I stumbled upon this quote: "…engineers create the world that never was." Immediately, it clicked: this is exactly what I had been doing throughout my many early years of gadget-fixing. When my undergraduate professor told me about a program where I could have two bachelor's degrees (one being a degree in engineering within five years), it sounded like a great deal. I'd eventually end up trading in this deal to pursue a PhD.

The time had finally come for me to decide if I was going to commit to the qualifying exam, or if I was going to use my CAPD diagnosis as an excuse to bow out gracefully. I mean, really, maybe all this was just a sign that the PhD journey wasn't for me. In any case, I could still get my master's degree and start working even earlier.

The only problem was that this decision wasn't

solely my own. It had mainly stemmed from doubt, which was brought on by individuals who amplified my concerns. With nothing to hold on to this time to keep me afloat, I agreed. Why put myself in a position where failing would break my confidence?

When I reflect on that moment, I wonder why it was so easy for me to relinquish all my power to those who wouldn't have to live with my decision. I can't say for sure where the confidence to return to my PhD program came from, but I do recall asking myself, "Why would I fail, just because I have a disorder?" This was followed by, "Why would I lose all self-worth, even if I failed?"

That was when I realized that as a Black woman in graduate school, our presence is very much an uncommon occurrence and we must mentally fight through not only our doubts, but the doubts of others. We have enough people projecting their thoughts and opinions on us; we can't afford to assume them onto ourselves.

Somehow, in the middle of all the mayhem and decision making, I knew there was still one more person I needed to talk to: my mother. Growing up in a Caribbean family, academic excellence was the only direction. Failure wasn't an option.

My mother had been my biggest advocate when it came to me studying internationally. She believed that seeing the world from a different perspective and being immersed in a different culture would allow me to be successful anywhere in the world. This was partly why it was so difficult for me to even think about making a call that I knew would disappoint her.

As the phone rang, I held my breath. Before she could even say "hello," I unloaded. I started with the feelings of frustration and the many challenges I was facing. Then, I went on to explain the options available, all while reassuring her that the shorter path was best. I only stopped when I realized she hadn't said a single word since she picked up the phone. I waited for her reaction with one eye closed, my left ear braced for a tongue lashing. Seconds of silence felt like hours before she finally responded in the calmest voice.

"So, basically, what you are saying to me is that you are taking the easy route? It sounds to me like you have already let others convince you of what you need to do. All I will say is, whatever you choose, make sure it is a decision that you have prayed about. There is only one chance. No do-overs. If you are okay with that, then you have my full support."

I realized she was right. I was no longer sure if what I said and felt was true, or a combination of everything I was being told. When you hear something enough times, you just tend to believe it.

Before I called my mother, walking away seemed to be the easiest thing to do. At that point, I didn't think I had the fight that was needed to get through this program. But like most mothers, she was right. I needed to decide what I thought I was truly capable of. I knew that if I was going to walk away, it was because I chose to—not because somebody made me. I was going to walk away only after exhausting every option, and only if I knew there was truly no place for me. I thought about those who would come after me, and their need for someone to believe in them (or at least hold the door open so they could follow behind).

Once my mother and I ended our call that evening, I decided that I was the only person who was going to be in control.

THE TRIBE

Something about that call with my mother made me realize that I was alone in this brand-new world of endless opportunities. Though her calls always meant the world to me, they weren't always enough. On heavy days, you need your loved ones to sit beside you, hold your hand, and tell you that even though the day sucked, you are still going to kick ass tomorrow.

In high school, I was accustomed to seeing my family at least once a week. It was a privilege I know many others didn't have. Even during my time in undergrad, I lived down the hall from people I could confide in. On the days I was really homesick, I knew that a break was never too far away. Those days would be followed by a short flight to Trinidad, even if it was just for a short break.

But in graduate school, not having my family nearby was beginning to become an unshakable burden. I was so busy struggling with classes and graduate life that regular calls were difficult to maintain. My class schedule and research hours always seemed to leave me with free time in the middle of the night, when the rest of the world was asleep.

Suddenly, you find that you are no longer a permanent fixture in people's lives. I was disappointed to know that I was no longer a go-to person for my friends, and I began to feel us drifting apart. The long distance made it increasingly difficult for me to feel as though I was still needed, even in the smallest way. The check-ins were no longer regular. Why would they be? We were all leading different lives, and though I couldn't quite grasp the change, I empathized. When it came to life events or family drama, I was even more disconnected. I didn't need the distraction, but sometimes a bit of "tea" was exactly what I needed to get me through the week. If anything happened, I found out much later; if I happened to hear about it immediately, I felt useless. It seemed like it was time for me to find a new circle in the place I now called home.

When I thought of home, I thought of growing up constantly surrounded by family. My father had ten siblings. My mother had seven. I never had to find a circle—I was blessed to be born into one. Even though some of my aunts and uncles were fifty years my senior, I grew up attending tea parties and nursing functions with my grandmother and my father's oldest sister. Being raised in a culture where everyone is considered family, you were always surrounded by a village—and that village was yours until the very end. Having a score of aunts and uncles and about two dozen cousins made the availability of someone to lean on almost inevitable. In my new normal, I was completely alone. The village that I once knew couldn't be the in-person tribe I needed. This was one major change I never had to face until graduate school.

On the first day of high school, I effortlessly walked up to the person who would turn out to be my best friend and asked, "Why yuh sitting alone?" Immediately, she became a part of my support system that believed in me and saw my gifts before I even recognized them myself. In that moment, I had made a lifelong friend.

But here I was, already halfway through the first semester, and I had yet to make a single friend or feel connected to anyone who understood what I was going through. To be frank, I probably wasn't trying hard enough, either. I would attend classes and then head directly home. Most days I was too tired from the academic mental beating to chat. Over time, I realized that you get what you put into it. Unfortunately, when you attend a predominantly white institution, a tribe isn't waiting for you on day one. You must seek it out, knowing that anything of substance is worth the work. I started with the only class where there was another person who looked like me. That moment changed my life forever. She was the first step to finding my tribe. I was invited to a student organization meeting that she thought might give me the sense of community I was longing for.

I remember thinking that I had never seen so many Black STEM students in one room. Even in my small undergraduate program, the physics department had very few Black physics majors. I felt like I was in a room surrounded by unicorns, as this wasn't the norm. It most certainly had never been portrayed by the media. I wondered where all these individuals were hiding on my first day. Immediately, I was welcomed into what I would soon learn was the NSBE (National Society of Black Engineers) family.

It felt great to be a part of a group that understood the feelings that came with attending the institution. They understood my stories of microaggressions; for instance, I told them how I felt the need to travel with my university sweater. When I didn't have it on, I was treated differently. They understood the surprised looks and countless times someone would tell me I "must be a smart girl" when I mentioned I was on the path to earning a PhD.

Not only did I find my tribe, but I found a greater support system than I could have ever imagined. They were a group of other minority graduate students who felt as flustered as I did and spent their weekends on campus due to their own never-ending list of tasks and experiments. To put it simply, this group offered me a safe space with study groups, conferences, late night hangouts, job interviews, experiments, and so much more. We all did what we had to do, and we did it together. We made sure that everybody stayed on track. If one person began to slip, another was there to grab hold and pull them back up.

A whole new world had opened up for me. I became a member of NSBE and found that the best way to break up the monotony of graduate school life was to be involved. Committing was a challenge at first, but it was one that I welcomed with open arms. It was nice to have my stress be focused on something different for a change. My second year was spent building these networks and growing them across campus and in the community. Nothing made me happier than giving back, and the distraction aided in getting me from "here we go again" to "let's get it done!"

On the journey to find your tribe, you may stumble on romance—but I wouldn't be keeping it real if I didn't put this out there: dating, in general, is hard. Dating in graduate school is harder! It sucked for me, anyway. They say, "Don't bring sand to the beach," but I should have brought an ocean's worth. Everyone is so busy trying to graduate and simply survive that very few are trying to put any real effort into a relationship. This is heightened when you attend a school in a rural area. My advice? Be strategic about how you pick someone to date. Apparently, there is a method to this madness.

If you date someone in your first year and their program is only two years long, there is no way to guarantee your future. Complications arise when you still have three years left and your partner is on their way out. I experienced this twice! I know you're thinking that if they really wanted to make it work, they would have. And, to some extent, that is true. However, there are so many unknown factors that make it difficult to want to commit.

THE BUDGET

After you've found your tribe (and possibly a little romance), you'll want to spend time together. If you're like me and you are attending school in a remote location, fellowship over a good meal will happen more often than it probably should. Remember that for many, graduate school is a financially challenging time. Everyone says that college is where we gather some of our biggest debt, but I feel as if I must reiterate that sentiment. This is where a larger portion of my credit card debt was accumulated.

There were times when my car would suddenly need service, and the repair fee was more than my fortnightly income. Even though I was older and could move my schedule around for much-needed me time (if you don't, you better), I also wasn't financially able to splurge on myself. It was difficult to treat myself on a budget. Hell, it was difficult to have a budget at all. But I had to try. There were a few strategies that helped me and a few things I wish I had done differently, especially when it came to financial freedom. I want you to bear these things in mind:

- If you can afford it, pay towards the interest on your student loans. Loan forgiveness plans can help you dissolve your student debt, but not everyone is able to qualify. I started paying back my student loans during my first year of graduate school, mainly because of a careless clerical error. My lender hadn't realized that I was still enrolled as a full-time student. So, they sent a bill right on schedule—six months after my undergraduate matriculation. For one year, I paid the full monthly payment (if I understood more about the process, I would have just paid interest), which was an obvious financial constraint. In hindsight, it worked out. Even though it was an unexpected expense, I was able to decrease my loan by a significant portion by the time I graduated. I was paying the interest towards my student loans, and once tax season rolled around, I was able to recoup thanks to the interest previously paid.

- Save what you can! Expenses come up all the time, and most of the time, they come without warning. As I mentioned before, part of my credit card debt came from car repairs. The rest was due to other simple, everyday purchases. If I was able to commit to saving at least twenty dollars a week, I would have been able to go on my dream vacation as soon as I was awarded my PhD instead of a year later. There are so many ways to start saving, including saving challenges with friends, bank withdrawal limits, investment mobile apps, and the good ole piggy bank method. Whichever method you choose, make sure that you are consistent. Can you imagine if you saved twenty dollars a week, every week, throughout graduate school? Whether you decide to travel, save for your post-graduate transition, or pay bills, it is yours to keep for that rainy day.

- Learn how to cook. This one is a toss-up; years ago, food was less expensive. Now, you can eat out almost daily at a reasonable price, and still spend the same amount of money as you would on a grocery haul. But why not cook and bring the fellowship to the house? Rotate where it is hosted and make it a potluck. This way, everyone contributes, but the bill is nowhere near as high as it would have been if ten people went out to a restaurant together.

TAKING THE EXAM AND PASSING

Once I found my tribe, I knew someone would be there to either hold my hand as I walked into the examination room or hold my hand as I walked away for good. By the end of my first semester, I had come to terms with my CAPD diagnosis but still had my insecurities about people noticing what may seem like lack of knowledge.

The day of the qualification exam finally arrived. The lack of sleep from the night before left me feeling fear and doubt, but mostly, I just wanted it to be over. I kept going over the list in my head of everything I had studied. I needed all bases to be covered. I fought so hard for my six-month extension that I knew I had something to prove.

I had spent the entire Christmas break preparing for this exam, and the semester before that auditing classes. Auditing undergraduate courses, even when it wasn't required, was the sacrifice I made to secure my place in the PhD program. It provided me with the foundation I knew I had previously lacked when I was first expected to take the exam.

As I walked into the exam room, I knew that I had to let go of my anxieties about being the "only one" in a room. These were feelings I had whenever I thought about "doing it for my race." I didn't have the privilege of failing, especially since I had already delayed the exam six months before. For the few hours of the exam, I reminded myself of how hard I had worked to get there. It was about showing the beauty of my mind.

I needed to quickly put walls up and keep my thoughts on mute. Since it was an oral exam, it meant that I had to really pay attention to the questions as they were being asked. The learning method I used for my CAPD had only been applied to reading, so this was going to be the first time I would be using it to try to visualize the problem as it was being asked. Risky, I know. As I turned to the board to begin solving, I felt every eye in the room dissect my every move. While I tried my hardest to remember the question, a wave of nervousness overcame me. Rather than become deterred, I confidently asked for the question to be repeated. This time, I did my visualization aids on the board and accompanied them by lopsided drawings and scribbles. There was no indication from their faces whether I was solving the problem correctly or making a complete fool of myself. Before I knew it, a wave of more questions came rushing in.

After wrapping up the final question, I was quietly dismissed. Instead of being asked to wait for the committee's results, as was customary, I was told that I would receive a call later that day or the next morning. It was already six o'clock; I had been in there for well over two hours.

Everything after that moment felt like a blur. I drove home on autopilot and didn't realize I had made it all the way to my highway exit until the buzzing of my phone snapped me back to reality. There I was, waiting on the turn signal, when the administrative office called. I knew that the conversation was either going to open a new path or destroy the life I was beginning to envision for myself. I wondered if I should pull over, but before I could decide, I heard the most beautiful two words: "You passed." Hearing those words was a relief. The first phase was done. I was exhilarated. Those would be the first of many major, happy tears I would shed on this journey. Things were finally starting to turn around for me, and I couldn't be happier.

THE ASSISTANTSHIP

With the right tools, it was much easier to understand my classes. My newfound method forced me to not just learn the subject matter, but really absorb it.

The strategy came at the right moment, because I was now officially a teaching assistant (TA) for the second semester. This meant that I was balancing both classes and teaching assistant responsibilities. This may not be the case with all programs, but my program required me to be a TA for two semesters. If you have never been a TA before, this is an opportunity to get experience without being a full professor. As a TA, I was tasked with instructional responsibilities like grading papers, all while maintaining office hours and lab sessions for undergraduate students. I felt as if every year of my PhD journey was an upward battle.

However, the TA experience is a great lesson in patience and preparation. The experience ensured that I used my learning tools for myself more than ever before. For every question a student asked, I had to make sure I understood it completely before I could truly explain the concept, especially since they hung onto my every word. This also meant that I was partly responsible for someone's interpretation of a topic; the last thing I needed was misinterpreted concepts.

Even though passing my exam had boosted my

confidence, I couldn't help but feel like a fraud every time I stood at the front of the classroom. I had imposter syndrome. This was something I had experienced from day one. I feared that those around me would question my knowledge of a given topic, but even worse, I had an immense fear of failure. I had worked my ass off and had the accolades to show for it, but it was a feeling I just couldn't easily shake. This would go on to be something that I would battle throughout my PhD program, my career, and beyond.

The only way I learned to overcome my imposter syndrome was to figure out the cause. In my case, it was my confidence in the subject. The more I understood it, the better I became at answering every harrowing question that came my way. I also used periodic check-ins with my advisor to discuss my progress.

To really ensure I was on track to mastering the subject matter for the classes I was taking, I became homework partners with the only other Black woman I saw in class. Even though we only took one class together, we found relief in seeing representation in each other especially within the same department. We understood each other's thought process when it came to our experiences, and found relief in discussing the challenges we endured and how to confront them.

We were the perfect mix of direct and passive, with me being the latter. With her in my corner, I was finally feeling at home in this once foreign space. Things got even better when I was able to hire her as one of my research students in the lab.

As expected, she excelled, and reminded me a lot of myself in the way she approached given tasks. It was almost like she went into survival mode, and success could only be measured when she excelled beyond the intended results and completed the program. With another person of color on my team, especially a Black woman, I felt a type of confidence I never had before. She never looked at me with skepticism when I gave directions and trusted my expertise without question. Though she only worked with the team for one semester, she was truly the catalyst towards self-assurance.

THE RESEARCH

The rest of the year seemed hazy as I struggled with balancing classes, being a teaching assistant, and trying to figure out what my research topic was going to be. What did I like? What could I see myself working on for five or six years? It would have to be something that I would remain motivated by if I had to read about it every single day.

Watching others conduct their research made me feel like finding my research area would be a breeze. They all seemed so engrossed and passionate by the work that they were doing. When you think about research, you think of reading an array of topics to help you develop something new. As a new student, you especially try to figure out what could take no more than five years (give or take a couple) to accomplish. After all, your plan may be to get in and get out of graduate school, but without a clear plan, the open-ended nature of research can create an endless abyss that exists until what may seem like the end of time.

Committing to a research topic required deep thought, and I decided to be open to everything. That was my first mistake. When my advisor asked me to pick a project, I was just excited to finally get my feet wet. The first step was getting familiar with the topic I had initially chosen and teaching myself the basics. There is no user guide to research, and since this was all new, I felt myself become increasingly flustered as

I got deeper and deeper. The more background research I did, the more I had to research additional information in order to understand what I had just read. It was becoming a labyrinth of information, and I was beginning to feel trapped.

After a few tries, I realized that I didn't enjoy a single thing about the topic. In my head, research was about making sure that I found a topic I would enjoy learning about every day. Even if I didn't like it some days, I would still want to learn more. That first summer never produced that feeling. The problem now was finding a way to tell my advisor that the topic I had chosen wasn't for me. It felt like, once again, I was going to disappoint him. Instead of dealing with the embarrassment of letting him down, I spent the entire summer researching a topic I knew would never make me happy. While I have no regrets, I do wish I had spoken up sooner. If I did, my summer could have been spent reflecting on exactly how I might contribute towards my field.

By the end of August, I knew that if I didn't speak up soon, I would be tied to this topic for the rest of my PhD journey. My lack of attachment made it clear that any work I produced would be half-hearted. The one thing you don't want to do as you set forth towards a PhD is deliver work you aren't proud of. Your goal is to work towards something that has a lasting effect and moves the research forward.

Is there a more awkward moment than admitting your research topic is an absolute bust? If there is, I have yet to encounter it. We convince ourselves that the failed topic will eventually grow on us, because the last thing we want is to be seen as "too much trouble" or unappreciative of the opportunity afforded to us. The truth is, we *have* worked our asses off to be in these spaces, and for that reason alone, we must do everything with clear intentions and make every moment count.

I didn't know what the repercussions of changing my research path would be, if any. But I knew that I couldn't spend another moment pretending to learn something I didn't enjoy. I learned an important lesson after I told my advisor my true feelings. He said, "From the moment you realized that this particular focus wasn't for you, you should have said something. We research and we explore to find our niche, but it doesn't mean that you stick with the first thing you're exposed to."

He reminded me of the power I had and the fact that he was there as *my* advocate, and not the other way around. Too often we allow fear to lead us away from the things that we deserve. Despite the many times this may have been questioned or challenged throughout history, let us never forget that we are deserving of the best education and support systems there are. We need not fear owning and amplifying our voices. I just had to figure out what I was truly willing to commit myself to.

The idea for my research topic came about randomly while my advisor and I were in the office discussing our respective childhoods. This topic of conversation wasn't uncommon for us, and it was nice to take a break to discuss the different island cultures by which we were raised. I was complaining that my first summer in upstate New York was so hot and humid compared to the dry heat we had back home in Trinidad. I talked about the breeze that made my paradise cool at night, no matter how warm the day had been. I explained that the capital was on the waterfront, and that you could catch a ferry to travel between the twin isles.

Before I knew it, we were brainstorming different ways we could take advantage of the incoming wind at the waterfront to ensure that the city became more sustainable. And just like that, in a matter of minutes and a few words, I had discovered my research problem. It amazed me how researchers dove in headfirst, not knowing if a problem would yield any productive results. Now I was one of them, and exceptionally proud of it.

It seemed as though the easy part was deciding on a research topic. The real work was coming up with a plan on how to make it a reality.

YEAR TWO LESSONS

BUILD A NETWORK

Even if you are an introvert and love time alone, it is important to have a space to crawl into—especially on the long days when you need to escape but don't wish to do so alone.

If it is difficult for you to find your people through your daily routine, get involved. There are student clubs, community outreach groups, and activities you can attend and get involved with. Before you say no, allow yourself to try at least one. Your only regret will be not trying sooner.

I found support in the diversity office for engineering students and in the diversity and inclusion department, which was available through the graduate school office. Seeking support is difficult, especially when you aren't sure where to look. Never be too afraid to ask questions about support offices for minority students, and seek out groups that are specific to minority groups and people of color. I was able to find student organizations, as well as my sorority's chapter.

Always keep your family close. Finding a tribe will not and should not replace your family. Though distance can cause disconnect, especially when you are hundreds or thousands of miles away, it's your responsibility to stay intertwined. It is easy to recede into your own world with the stress of hard deadlines and extracurricular commitments. Doing so, however, only makes challenging situations seem impossible to overcome, especially during moments that call for a familial touch.

COMMIT TO THE RIGHT RESEARCH TOPIC

Once you land on a topic, it is either going to pique your interest or leave you empty and craving more. Find something that fuels your fascination more than it sparks frustration. The goal is to find a topic that reflects graph A.

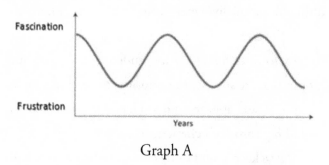

Graph A

If you find yourself more frustrated than fascinated over time, as shown in Graph B, then it may be time to rethink your research. It could mean adding an extra research element, or rethinking something that's already included. Frustration will happen, but it should be well-balanced with your yearning to move the needle in the subject area further.

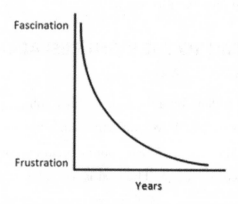

Graph B

BE OPEN ABOUT YOUR IDEAS

We have all been told that there are no dumb questions. Well, I believe the same goes for ideas: no idea is too dumb. There will always be one that fits immediately with the problem you are trying to solve. Don't be afraid to share your ideas with your advisor or your committee. You can gauge their feedback to figure out if it is a wholesome idea or not. Be creative and let your mind flow. You never know—you may have an intellectual property (IP) treasure on your hands.

DO YOUR RESEARCH

When it comes to research, you need to make sure that you always stay in the loop within the field. This means finding what has been done in the topic you chose and what has been recently attempted. Sometimes your idea may have already been done, which can save you from preforming unnecessary tasks. Always make sure you are up-to-date on current popular journals in your field. Consider setting an alert for new publications, or simply doing a quick internet search (e.g. "scholar" or JSTOR) every so often.

NO INVENTION? NO PROBLEM.

As new graduate students, we enter the research phase of our journey ready to change the world and, hopefully, accomplish something groundbreaking. We often feel the pressure to come up with something that is completely novel. We fail to realize that just because we don't invent something new, it doesn't mean that we can't innovate. Advancing the field doesn't mean that you need to think of a completely new concept. In this instance, it can mean advancing the field one or more steps beyond where it was, or adding something new to the existing field. It can also include expanding on someone else's research by unlocking a previously unexplored concept. Whichever lane you choose, know that your contributions are just as valuable as creating something new. Remember, research can only get recognized if others can continue to explore what has been done and build upon it.

Advance the field by allowing your mind to be innovative. Your PhD success is determined by your gained subject matter expertise and how well you can articulate it.

NO ONE LOVES A "YES" QUEEN

We have all had moments where we have agreed to do something we absolutely didn't want to do. In those cases, who really cared to notice the inflection in our voices as we regrettably took on a task? I guarantee no one notices, or, quite frankly, even cares. People are not going to know unless you outrightly express your displeasure. Professors don't have the time to observe your reaction to a question or note the changes to your demeanor. It is perfectly okay to respond by asking for some time to think it through. This gives you time to evaluate if you have the capacity to take on the request, and lets others know that you truly considered what was asked of you.

END OF CHAPTER WORKSHOP

What communities can I join to build my network?

_____

_____

_____

_____

_____

_____

How do I find my tribe?

_____

_____

_____

_____

_____

_____

What am I looking for in a tribe?

_____

_____

_____

_____

_____

_____

What are some events I can attend to seek out the tribe I am looking for?

_____

_____

_____

_____

_____

_____

How can I create a safe-space for myself?

_____

_____

_____

_____

_____

_____

MONEY TALKS

Use the table below to help you track your monthly spend. Building out a simple budget will help you to stay on track.

My Stipend: _____

Budget Breakdown

ITEM	COST
Rent	
Utilities (include wifi and cable, if applicable)	
Food	
Transport-Public/Private (include insurance if applicable)	
Savings (Min $50)	
Miscellaneous item #1	
Miscellaneous item #2	
Miscellaneous item #3	
Miscellaneous item #4	

YEAR THREE

"Thinking you can is one thing, but knowing you can gets you halfway there."

– Dr. Malika Grayson

The halfway point of any journey can be just as satisfying as it is discouraging. For me, the third year was my halfway point. It was also the year I was committed to doing whatever it took to make it across that finish line. Though I was focused and up for the task, two words would follow me around for most of that year: "criticism" and "self-confidence." In the third year, I had to learn to control my emotions when it came to receiving criticism. When you have placed all bets on something, you become very protective of it. Disappointment often stems from knowing how much effort was placed into our work, only to have it discredited in mere minutes. Learning how to use the criticism I received in a way that enhanced my overall project was key to my third-year success.

It might sound like I was a bit late in the game, but this was a good year for me to really evaluate my self-confidence. It was especially important now that I was a senior member of my lab and students reported directly to me. I could no longer allow imposter syndrome to stay in my thoughts rent-free; every moment I questioned myself, I made it easier for others to scrutinize my work. Whether it was the students who attended my office hours or my lab students who looked to me for confirmation, I needed to exude confidence with every explanation I gave and with every problem I resolved.

THE THIRD YEAR PLAN

One of the best things about starting my third year was knowing that I finally had a research area. Although I knew there was a small possibility of it changing (because every graduate student knows you can't breathe until you start producing actual results), I was looking forward to learning more. For once, I felt connected to my topic and envisioned myself, years from now, bringing new technology to the country that had nurtured my inquisitive mind. The question was, where should I start?

I realized that I also needed to have a plan for how I researched. Where was my focus going to be, and how broad of a research topic did I want to cover? I didn't want to bite off more than I could chew, but I also didn't want to take on too narrow of a topic. As a graduate student, you always want to appear to be more than just capable of scratching the surface of a topic. It was important that I was committed, because by the end of my third year, I was expected to take the admission to candidacy exam. Yup, another exam.

But more on that later.

Even though I had concrete goals for the future of my research, I still felt as though I was last place in a race. I eventually realized this race only included myself. While I had spent my first year learning all there was to know about general engineering topics, I spent the first half of my second year preparing for the graduate program's qualifying exam. Once that was over, I spent the second half of the year being a teaching assistant. When I entered my third year, I was expected to teach during the first semester once again. It was safe to say that I would be starting the year on fumes.

Although I enjoyed the experience of being a teaching assistant, I also had no choice. I came into my graduate program with only my first year of funding fully secured. Though I applied to PhD fellowships for funding every year, I always managed to receive an honorary mention. This put immense pressure on us to find funding. If I was unable to find funding for the remainder of graduate school, I would have to be a teaching assistant until the day I crossed the stage.

The teaching assistantships were based on availability and the classes that needed assistance, and always ended up being a great financial back-up plan. Though it removed some financial strain, it also meant that I would have less time to focus on my research, since the assistantship required about twenty hours per week.

Thankfully, my TA back-up plan came in handy for the first semester of my third year. However, I needed to integrate the extra hours it required into my plan for year three. The first part of the plan was ensuring I signed up for courses that could help me gain more background knowledge on my research topic. After taking my class hours into consideration and adding research hours in between my mandatory TA hours, I finally felt ready to start off the semester on the right foot (or at least pretend to). With my new schedule, I barely had a second to breathe. Year three was shaping up to be the most challenging yet.

Here are a few tips to consider when you are planning for year three:

- Research what has been done in the field, and do some further leg work on understanding what solutions may have been limited.

- When you find gaps in the research, consider how you plan to fill them. Remember, a big part of this is time management.

- As a full-time student—especially if you are a teaching assistant—you can't do everything by yourself. This is the time to speak up and ask your advisor for help. It is your advisor's job to ensure that you have the resources available to you. In my case, this came in the form of undergraduate and master's students.

- Remember to set goals. Short-term goals will help break down bigger tasks. This may mean setting weekly goals to tackle and planning everything on your impending schedule.

- Remember to find balance. Sometimes we plan and execute so well that we forget to plan time for ourselves. Breaks are important even when they are hard to come by. If you don't find time for breaks (going to the gym, taking a walk, or a night off), you are more than likely going to experience burnout. Many students, including myself, have been there because we refused to listen to our bodies. We beat ourselves up because we feel guilty for not working all the time. We are often conditioned to believe that rest is synonymous with laziness; when you have something to prove in graduate school, this notion is only amplified.

THE SPIRITUAL CHECK-IN

It was during my morning commute on the bus when I saw her. There she was, as calm as ever—just praying. Even with the incessant chatter of the morning rush, she remained laser-focused on her Qur'an. She appeared so peaceful and centered in spite of it all. I admired her, and may have harbored a bit of envy towards her. It made me think about my own spirituality, and I realized I hadn't stepped into a church in over a year. I wondered if my stressful days would be a little less challenging if I started my mornings off, like she did, within a sea of stillness.

It may sound cliché, but before this point, I didn't fully believe in the power of prayer. We all say that people only pray when times get tough, but is that not how faith works? It's after our lowest points when we cry the loudest and make promises we know that we can never keep.

My father's family has been attending the same church for decades, and several of my cousins and I had been christened there. Even though I came from a praying family, where both my grandmothers prayed multiple times a day, my prayers were never as frequent. When I did attempt to pray, it often got monotonous. I am sure you know exactly what I mean. When your heart is not truly in it, it gets to the point where it all sounds rehearsed and false.

I sat on my couch later that night, trying to plan the two semesters ahead. I surprised myself—and quite honestly, scared myself—by the frustrated scream I let out. It contained months of distress as I tried to grapple with my new sense of reality. I needed to find hope and believe that there was going to be a way to make it through.

Religion is always a sensitive subject, because we all have our opinions on who we should pray to. Some of us are even ashamed to claim our religion, or are ashamed to pray because we don't want to be seen. But in graduate school, you can't afford to be ashamed or shy—there are too many other things to worry about! When we overthink religion and its meaning in our lives, we overlook the fact that it is less about someone's religion and more about having an outlet that gives you hope and replenishes your faith. I, for one, was going to need all the replenishment I could get.

While exploring ways I could define a new relationship with prayer, I also found a sense of community with people who would join me in giving thanks. Often, I would go to church and sit in the back without saying a word. I would "do my penance," as they say, feeling satisfied that I could now get through my week. For me, it was about finding solace in a place where I could have an open conversation about my faith, or even question life without judgement or curious eyes. I wanted to spend time asking the questions that I didn't know the answers to: Why did this path choose me? Why was this journey a daily struggle, with no end in sight? If things were this difficult now, was it still meant to be?

I can't tell you why you should pray or why others do, but I can tell you why I did. As I mentioned earlier, this was one of the most difficult years throughout my program. Every day came with frustrations that made me want to shed a few tears: not knowing the solutions to my problems; failed experiments; and mostly, exhaustion. My spirituality was the one thing that helped me escape. It provided me with the ease of knowing that through my newly reinforced faith, I could get through anything.

THE NITTY-GRITTY

Even with my renewed spirituality, I was going to have to dig deep to get through the next phase of my journey. By my second semester, the heavens smiled down on me, as I no longer needed to be a teaching assistant. My advisor had been working on a grant, which was finally awarded. This meant that I could finally have a semester that focused solely on my research.

This blessing couldn't have come at a better time. When I started planning out my year, I failed to realize just how much work it took to get a research project up and running while also producing consistent results. I had to know everything from the right equipment to purchase to what results I wanted to deliver. To figure this out, I had to continually run various experiments, which meant I couldn't do it alone. I had to reconcile with the fact that asking for help didn't mean I was incompetent. What it really meant was that I wanted to succeed in the most thorough way possible. After meeting with my advisor, we agreed that it was best to bring on two new students, in addition to three students who had previously worked in our lab.

For some reason, this pending responsibility made me more nervous than being a teaching assistant. Here I was, the double-minority team leader, in charge of five young men whose grades and credits depended on how well I was able to explain, delegate, and advise. Not to mention I literally had my whole PhD career riding on how well we were able to work as a team. They could tell I had never done this before, and were hesitant to follow my lead. The students who had worked in our lab already had their leader, and were accustomed to certain expectations. I wondered if they would respect me as a team leader, especially when there were no other women or people of color on the team.

At first, I struggled with leading the team. I kept holding back out of fear of coming off too harsh or aggressive. Society sees Black women as emotional and brash when we voice our opinions, and I didn't want to deal with giving in to dated stereotypes. I knew that at some point, I needed to refocus on the role I held in relation to theirs. It dawned on me that whether they were successful or not, I—the only

Black woman in the room—would be held responsible.

For that reason, it was difficult to rely on others to complete tasks on my behalf. My need to convey that this space was one that I had rightfully earned made me believe that each task was solely my own to complete. I was so accustomed to fighting for a place to fit in that I forgot the point was to hold a space for us all to thrive—especially me. If I kept this going, there would be no team or project to oversee.

I struggled to find the balance between being passive and overly assertive while demanding what I needed from them. Eventually, I realized that whether they had done something wrong or gotten it perfectly right, I would always be held responsible. I had to aim for my intended results, regardless of how I appeared.

It is important to always keep in mind that this is your project; don't be afraid to hover. Scratch that—hovering in the beginning is important. Letting go of the reins before your students are truly ready could result in setbacks.

One way to ensure that you trust what your students are doing is to ask them "why." Why do they think the results are the way they are? Or, why should the equipment be set up in that manner? Asking these questions is not just about making sure they get it right, but ensuring they understand the essential attributes of the project. It shows that your interest is beyond them doing the work and more inclusive of their learning. I often got the best support from undergraduate students when I treated them as my team members, rather than my subordinates.

Once I found my rhythm, it felt like I could finally focus my attention on results until both my advisor and I believed I was ready to take my admission to candidacy exam. Like my qualifying exam, this was another comprehensive exam to assess my readiness. This time, the goal was to assess my readiness for the dissertation process and to ensure my research was meaningful and grounded enough to contribute to the field.

Most graduate students in my lab had taken the exam in their fourth year. If I were to do the same, it would allow me just enough time to formulate a cohesive story for my research project. At that point, I was less worried about my hectic schedule, as I knew my first year of research didn't truly start until the end of my second year.

When the department announced that it would be upholding the rules that required all third-year graduate students to have the exam completed by the end of their third year, I was in utter distress. It was already midway through the second semester. Just to get one graph to accurately reflect my research took two or three days of lab measurements. My end-to-end process included experimental measurements, which often took the most time. On good days, it took a few hours to measure data; on others, it took literal days.

The only thing worse than not having enough experiments done was finding a time when all my committee members could meet for my exam. It could end up being just as hard as the entire exam preparation process. Though I was literally running out of time, I had to find the best time for three busy professors to meet. I was hoping that their busy schedules would work in my favor. If we were unable to find a suitable time, I would have to delay my exam until everyone became available.

We were nearing the second half of the semester. Summer yielded the busiest time for professors, due to conferences and personal responsibilities. Normally, this would be a game-changer—but if you haven't figured it out by now, nothing throughout this experience came quite as easily as I would've liked. It seemed that there was no amount of time where I would feel one hundred percent ready. If there is anything you can learn from my experience, it is that it is never too early to plan!

The admission exam date depends on circumstances. You choose the date, but you never want to be caught off guard. By the time I made the twenty rounds to find the perfect date, it was scheduled for June 24.

Let's think about this for a minute. The conversation I had with my advisor about the admission exam took place sometime in March. Normally, there would be ample time to get prepared; instead, I had less than two months to ensure I had done enough to secure the future of my research.

The best way for me to approach the tasks that lay ahead was to map it all out on the actual slides I would present during the exam. This gave me an idea of what "chapters" of my research story I was still missing. It also meant that my experiments and overall timeframe would have to be ramped up, forcing me to lean heavily on my students. This was the point where I learned to trust myself.

I had to ensure everything was completed on time, and sleepless nights became second nature to me. I still remember one night when, after dauntingly running my results, I was ready to put down the pens and pencils and walk away for good. There were about two weeks left until my exam, and with the difficulty I had getting the results I expected, I was beginning to feel defeated.

It was around midnight when I felt my eyes begin to swell with tears. As anxiety quickly settled in my chest, I wanted nothing more than to scream and destroy every piece of apparatus I had in the lab. Everything—from the robotic arm that refused to work to the ladder I had to drag out every time I needed to climb on top of the wind tunnel and reset equipment—felt like it was breaking me down. At the time, I thought to myself, "I have never been so frustrated in my life." The only thing that was left to do was to burst into tears. I realized that this may not work out the way I wanted it to. And by "this," I meant my entire PhD plan.

THE FREEDOM TO BE VULNERABLE

In vulnerability, we can often find strength. It is in the times of our greatest loss that we see the answers that we need clearer than ever. Surprisingly enough, preparing for the admission to candidacy exam did just that. I was spending so much time trying to perfect my preliminary results that I had forgotten all about the bigger picture: What was my research story? What were the steps that followed my research? When would the field be impacted?

I had been a perfectionist when it came to completing tasks, but I still had some discomfort with the amount of vulnerability completing a PhD required—even in my third year. At each turn, this program revealed my every imperfection. Once I realized I couldn't solve all my research problems in one night, I decided to take what I had and began to build my story. There were various layers of my research and its purpose, but my story needed to show my committee that I had a solid plan, and that I was ready to do whatever it took to see it to fruition.

I knew how persistent I could be and had to give myself a deadline for running experiments. If I didn't, I would always try to run one more experiment, which would turn into five before I went home. At some point, we must accept the fact that our improvement curve plateaus with time, and the extra five percent of improvement isn't worth the additional effort.

I used the time I had left before the exam to meet with my committee regularly. I wanted to know more about their expectations and what questions I needed to answer. I tried to prepare as much as possible, but once the day came, it still felt as if I could use an extra month.

I remember how sweaty my palms were—to the point where it was difficult to hold the pointer. This was probably caused by the serious faces of each committee member that greeted me as I entered the room. The exam was open to the public, and my department had sent out an announcement to show their support. The only thing worse than presenting to people who were authorities on the topic was presenting it to a room full of complete strangers. It's funny; we often assume that our revolutionary idea is exactly what the world has been waiting for, but it only takes one person to make an unsolicited comment for us to feel like we should be doing more.

Believe it or not, the presentation wasn't the hardest part. Reality set in when everyone left the room and it was just the committee and me. That was when the real questions began. Be prepared to not know every answer. Most importantly, be ready for criticism. Every professor has an opinion and valid suggestions for improvement. But ultimately, you and your advisor have to decide which recommendations are best for your successful completion.

One of the committee's suggestions was that I

needed to spend at least a year reconfiguring my apparatus. My advisor, who had always been my first line of defense, had my back and knew it wasn't feasible given the time and funding I had left. This is the importance of having an advisor who is a vocal advocate of your work. He took the risk and responsibility to assure them that I didn't need the extra time as he would work alongside me to figure out how I could improve the results I already had. Improving meant that I needed to redo several of my experiments, but at least I knew what I was doing this time around. It was also suggested that I take a few more classes aligned with my research to increase my subject matter knowledge, and ultimately help me with the necessary research revisions.

It wasn't uncommon to take classes that helped your research, but it was uncommon for a fourth-year student to be doing so. Though it would be a slight blow to my ego, it was something I needed. So, I embraced it as one more thing that would get me closer to the "Phinish(D) Line."

By the time we got through all eighty slides, I had pages of opinions, recommendations, and changes to consider. At first, I thought that it was impossible—a ploy to get me to say, "No thanks." But if I could sit through an hour-long interrogation where three opinionated men debated what my next step should be, I would be able to handle any additional research adjustments they threw my way. I let go of my ego and took the criticisms (or "growth opportunities," as I call them now) they provided. When they were done, I asked for suggestions on improvement.

I found my voice and let them know that while there seemed to be a great deal left for me to do in a short period of time, I was ready. I told myself that I was taking back the power I had so easily handed over to who I thought held my future in their hands. All they held were pens to sign my form; regardless of which box they ticked, I was in control.

Guess what? They ticked the recommendation to pass. It was a conditional pass, due to the classes I needed to take—but hey, I was happy to take it! It was official: I was now a PhD Candidate.

YEAR THREE LESSONS

CHOOSE YOUR BATTLES

I once asked one of my mentors how he dealt with difficult faculty, he told me to choose my battles wisely. He said that if you have a valid point and a convincing argument, it can sometimes be good for you to tell your side—but usually, it is better to choose your battles. In other words, sometimes the battle just isn't worth the war that may follow. I found myself not accepting defeat, per se; just choosing to do what was needed to get to the next phase.

Part of choosing your battles is also being able to listen to the critiques that are given. Based on the feedback I got after my admission exam, I still had a long way to go—but I no longer felt defeated.

DEALING WITH DIFFICULT COMMITTEE MEMBERS

Sometimes, the PhD war is inevitable. The first thing you need to do is find an ally on your committee. Your most important ally should always be your advisor, but it also helps to have someone else on your committee in your corner. This is someone who understands your vision and is able to enhance it instead of diminish it.

We try to choose committee members that complement each other, your research topic, and the expertise you need; in most cases, that can be a bit hard to come by. For many of us, the only qualifying factor we get is someone in our field of study. We ignore the fact that we may only see this person three times in five years, because they hold something vital to the completion of our journey: a signature. It is important to try to establish a relationship with each of your committee members. This will help you understand what to expect and may make it easier to work through any difficult encounters.

YOUR PROJECT, YOUR MESS

There has never been a time when a team has lost a game and immediately claimed "Player X" was the sole cause. They say "Team A" was defeated. The same applies to your lab and the members of your team. If a mistake is made under your watch, it is your responsibility, no matter who was leading the task.

It is always a good idea to factor in accidental buffer time. Then, multiply that by two for when the accidental time just isn't enough. This can be applied to anything you are doing, be it an experiment (or data gathering), writing, or researching. In doing so, you avoid the anxieties of having to complete your project too close to your assigned deadline. It also gives you time to give your work your undivided attention and ensure it is also your best work being presented.

Remember to be reasonable with the time frame you choose. Be honest with yourself, your abilities, and the time required to accomplish your goals.

GIVE YOURSELF A PEP TALK

Amidst the hardships of year three, I found that reflective pep talks and words of affirmation can be calming during times of anxiety. The pep talk doesn't have to be long, but it should manifest the feeling you wish to attain.

OVERCOMING FUNDING WOES AND KNOWING WHERE TO TURN

The last thing you need to worry about in your third year, or any year, is funding. If funding is provided for the first year or two, the excitement can become a distraction. We forget that, eventually, the short-term funding runs out. Have a candid conversation with your advisor.

The conversation may be awkward, but your future security shouldn't be taken lightly. Ideally, this conversation should take place when you are interviewing with your advisor and determining if you are both a good fit for each other. One of the most important questions you can ask is, "What happens if a fellowship isn't rewarded?" You should also ask, "What is the contingency plan?"

1. REACH OUT TO YOUR DEPARTMENT

If you are having an issue with your advisor, reach out to the graduate department or diversity program in your school. As minority students, we tend to be afraid to speak up and forget that there are amazing resources available to us. At the beginning of my second year, it was important for me to have a conversation with the department's office. I needed to know about the contingency plan in the event there were no fellowships or grants available once I finished my semester as a teaching assistant. Conversations surrounding money will always be uncomfortable. These are the instances where your future takes precedence over your comfort zone.

2. TALK TO PAST AWARDEES

This is something I wish I did more often, just to really see what a winning package looked like. I was too ashamed to ask, but that is a fear that you must quickly overcome. Find out what key elements they had in their package that made them stand out. If the awardee happens to be a mentor or someone you admire, you should also consider asking them to help you form your application.

3. LOOK FOR FUNDING OPPORTUNITIES SPECIFIC TO YOUR AREA OF STUDY

There will always be major fellowships that students apply to. Those are great, because you already know the prestige and competitiveness surrounding it. If you spend some additional time to look, you will also find that there are smaller grants (either general or specific to your field) that you can submit. These grants may be as simple as funding to a conference, or cash for a semester's worth of support. Nothing is too small, and no effort is too big when it comes to securing funding.

If the aforementioned funding isn't for you, you can choose to pursue the industry funding route. In this instance, a company chooses to sponsor the research of a PhD student. These sometimes come with requirements such as internships or specific research topics, which can put restrictions on what you focus on. But this can also be an incredible and unique opportunity that can open doors to so many things.

If this is something that you would be interested in, you should add it to your conversation with your advisor. Even before signing on to the lab, ask if they have industry connections and partners; this can be a great starting point.

END OF CHAPTER WORKSHOP

What are three questions I would like to answer with my research?

_____

_____

_____

_____

_____

_____

What will be my technique for taking criticism?

_____

_____

_____

_____

_____

What is one activity I will do for myself this year?

_____

_____

_____

_____

_____

YEAR FOUR

"You may encounter many defeats, but you must not be defeated. In fact, it may be necessary to encounter the defeats, so you can know who you are, what you can rise from, how you can still come out of it."

– Maya Angelou

ON CLOUD 9

Summer sessions were always when I was most productive. With classes out, everyone always seemed to be in great spirits. The quiet our campus offered was a great contrast to any other time of year. This was probably also due to the many professors who travelled for conferences and family vacations. This was especially great, because it meant less awkward run-ins and small talk about projects.

In my opinion, the summer is one of the best times to accomplish tasks. Even my late nights in the labs were bettered by knowing that when I left, it would still be seventy degrees outside. Advisors were also off basking in the warm weather; you were lucky if you could find time in your advisor's busy schedule.

My advisor and I had made great strides after I passed my exam, and we were both on the highs of my success. The good news took a bit of pressure off, which gave us the opportunity to make summer plans. I felt great about our conversation and was especially excited to show him my progress once the semester started. I had spent most of the summer buckling down and getting things done.

I spent the last days of my third year making a new plan for my PhD candidacy. I knew what my committee really thought of my research project, and I needed to make sure that I did everything on that list. I didn't want to give them any reasons to question my candidacy, especially when it came to my dissertation defense. My defense was still more than two years away, but the admission to candidacy exam taught me that time seemed to move at an expedited pace.

Despite the impending stress, I still walked onto campus my first day back with a different type of confidence—the confidence of an expert who was perfecting her craft. I went in already knowing what I expected from my students, and for the first time, my voice didn't shake.

That semester saw another first for my academic journey: I was able to register for my very first technical conference. The opportunity to travel to a place I had never been and speak about a topic I genuinely enjoyed was exactly what I imagined the glamorous part of a PhD journey to be. Being a fourth year PhD candidate had presented a whole new reality for me.

As a new student, you often admire your professors and their ability to balance this fascinating lifestyle that involves endless travel and conferences.

Once you take a closer look, it becomes clear that this lifestyle isn't only extremely expensive, but the "care instructions" for this comfortable way of life were extremely complicated.

I had spent most of my PhD career thus far on my advisor's care team, observing his dedication to his students and how hard he worked to ensure top-notch facilities were available. He knew that without the worry of faulty equipment, we would be better equipped to focus solely on producing work we could be proud of. So, when I got invited to my first conference, I knew that this was a win for my entire team.

Being invited to my first conference had also given me the added motivation I needed to set my fourth-year plan in motion. Finally, on the other side of my candidacy exam, I had to start putting the pieces of my dissertation story together. I began with an outline to help me identify any gaps I still needed to fill. It felt great to be on top of things for once.

THE RUG PULL

When I think of someone who was able to do it all, I think of my advisor. He participated on conference boards and diversity committees, maintained industrial partners for our lab funding, and had over twenty students under his charge. At times I worried that I would slip between the cracks, but he always made sure that he was available for me. I had spent so much time trying to find someone I could trust with my future that I was especially excited to let him know how much I was kicking ass.

When I didn't see him for the first few days of the semester, I knew something was wrong. Drowning in curiosity, my lab mates and I were eventually informed that he had been committed to the hospital with an unknown medical condition. We were immediately overwhelmed with concern, but being the advisor he was, he expected us to keep working on our respective projects. He expressed to us that he was looking forward to even more progress upon his return.

To soothe our concerns, my lab mates and I sent a card. We wanted to do more, but we knew that he wouldn't want us to worry. He would also be disappointed to know that our concerns had kept us from working. Despite our better judgement, we returned to work, mainly to ensure that the only thing he would have to take care of was his inbox. Our lab was just like any family, and we were dividing and conquering whatever tasks were thrown our way. After all, we were sure he would be back giving orders in no time.

The worst kind of random calls are the ones you miss while you are asleep. That morning, I woke up to multiple missed calls from my lab colleagues. Somehow, I already knew what was waiting for me on the other end. Though the idea filled me with dread, I hit redial. As the phone rang, I wished that there would be no answer. My stomach lurched when I heard my lab colleague's cracking voice on the other line. My advisor had died before he ever got a chance to recover from his condition.

Something shattered inside of me, and my first instinct was that I needed to go to school. I strongly believe that timing is everything, and my aunt had just started her visit with me the day before. She didn't know it then, but her presence kept me from truly spiraling in that moment. I barely made it to my front door when reality finally hit me and I collapsed. I thought about his family; I thought about how I was going to tell my students who worked in our lab; and, selfishly, I thought about what this meant for my future.

In times of tragedy, we try to gravitate towards

the people who understand how we feel, because they are feeling the same way. My lab colleagues were the ones who would understand my anger, shock, and sudden sadness. I went straight to the lab. As if we were all thinking the same thing, my lab family embraced. And though this gesture had begun to pull me from the pits of the pain I felt, I needed more. I needed my tribe. These were the people who understood just how hard I had fought the system as a Black woman just to find someone I trusted not just as a mentor, but a sponsor. He was someone who I knew had my back, whether I was in the room or not.

My tribe was waiting for me when I walked into the campus offices that supported minority engineering students. It was as if they already knew what I needed. Many of them were stunned by the news that had spread across campus like wildfire. Many within the engineering department grappled with what to do next. This was unchartered territory for many of us, and I had a feeling it would take some time to even comprehend what a massive loss this was. In the meantime, I found consolation in the fact that I had a place where I could sit in my grief with people who welcomed my sea of emotions.

The following week was an emotional rollercoaster.

I wondered what was going to happen to our lab, and if there was a contingency plan for us. If there was, was it the type of plan I was going to be willing to move forward with? We all suddenly felt out of place, and I no longer knew if graduate school was the place for me. My struggles here began on the very first day, and I wondered if this was God's plan all along. Was I meant to go through the fire just to prove that I could handle anything? I know we never get more than we can bear, but in that moment, I wasn't sure I could take much more.

I began the semester feeling like I was on top of the world, and in a matter of the days, I was once again at rock bottom. How could I continue without my advisor? What would become of my PhD journey without him by my side? Who would fight the battles and the politics of it on my behalf? He deserved to bear witness to my accomplishments, and he deserved to see how much he had changed my life. There were so many choices I was now forced to make, and questions that desperately needed answers. But first, we needed to come together to celebrate his life.

The celebration of his life continued at his home, a place he had welcomed us into countless times for talks and get-togethers. His home had always felt so inviting, and this time I knew it would be for the last time—a reality I wasn't ready to face. What I loved most about his leadership was the family he created with us. Being there without him felt like a betrayal, but instead of spilling sorrow, we knew that he deserved to be remembered for the blessing he was to us all. By the time the comforting but emotionally draining day had ended, I dreaded telling his wife goodbye. I meant to offer her a few comforting words, but our roles reversed. She opened up about the times they had spoken about me. She shared stories of how proud he had been of me, and how much he loved dedicating his life to research and his students. She told me he wouldn't want us to stop, and to make sure, now more than ever, that we finished the race.

The first two weeks after his funeral flew by, and it was finally time to face reality and try to regain any sense of normalcy. All the class planning I had done was paused; mentally, I could no longer continue. This time, I couldn't muscle my way through feelings or be strong. I had witnessed the women in my family have insurmountable strength, no matter what my family was challenged with. The women were expected to be the emotional rocks—not just in my family, but also within the Black community. History has constantly showed us that Black women rarely seek help when it comes to their emotional well-being. This very notion riddled me with guilt as I felt myself getting swept away in my emotions. Though these feelings were new and complex, I also knew that advocating for my mental health was nothing to be ashamed of. In no way did taking a moment to pause make me weak. I was human, no matter how superhuman I sometimes felt.

I remember being devastated after my grandmother passed away. She had been my driving force to complete my undergraduate studies. Just as I did back then, I recognized I could no longer allow myself to drown in self-pity. The world was still spinning, and I was still a part of it—even with the loss and the uncertainty of it all. But my advisor's presence had eclipsed so much of my world. He had set me so safely on my course to the finish line, and it was challenging for me to now grab hold of the reins and take control.

Where would I begin to pick up the pieces? I had no idea where to begin to figure out my future as a PhD graduate. Before now, I had only seriously considered dropping out of school one other time, and that was at the end of my first year. My excuse for dropping out then seemed like child's play compared to what I was facing now. As I toiled with my decision, I remembered what my advisor's wife had said. I heard his voice in my head, telling me that I better not use him as an excuse to not finish what *we* had started.

The first thing I needed to do was talk to my department to figure out what their plan was. Did I still have funding? What about funding for the remaining years? Despite the many questions I had, it was becoming painfully clear that I needed to begin looking for an advisor all over again. I needed to either find someone who would be willing to pick up where my advisor had left off, or I would have to start all over.

The second option seemed daunting, and the fact that this could be the case for me and so many of my lab colleagues gave me an instant migraine. I wasn't sure if I wanted to start this journey all over again, but I prepared myself for the worst-case scenario. In times like this, your support system truly shows you that there is strength in numbers. They had my back, regardless of what I decided to do, and were willing to help me pick up the thousands of pieces this loss had left behind. Even with their support, the real question was if *I* was ready to pick up the pieces. No matter how many times I tried to glue it all together, I would always be missing something.

At the end of September, I realized that I hadn't attended a single class, despite the list of classes my committee had said I needed to attend after my exam. Not only did I need to take my time and carefully return to my routine, I was still conflicted about fulfilling new classes and other graduate requirements I wasn't sure I was going to finish.

My walls had disintegrated brick by brick. One of my committee members seemed to sense this, and reached out to me. This was a meeting I was dreading. It also seemed peculiar that he had chosen a coffee shop for our meeting, almost as if it were a cover to soften the blow of bad news. I built my strength to look him in the eye without tearing up, but his tone was one of comfort. He was concerned about how I was coping, and understood the predicament I was in. As he shared his story of loss and how difficult it was for him to move on, I knew that he really did have my interests at heart. That was when he made me a proposal. He offered to become my advisor for the remainder of my time at graduate school.

To my surprise, I didn't have to switch my research area. He was also going to ensure that we had a strategy in place to help me complete my research and graduate within the next few years. The kicker? He had already begun his retirement transition. Before that conversation, I wondered how I could rebuild years of trust in a matter of months. It suddenly became a non-factor. Here he was, willing to delay his retirement so I had someone to get me across that finish line. If that wasn't God, then I don't know what was.

The only real contingency was that everything needed to be completed by the end of my fifth year, both for funding purposes and his transition. I also needed to find an additional committee member, and my new advisor suggested I add a fourth. The more people in your committee, the better it is for you in terms of expertise and guidance. Once again, everyone had a different opinion regarding my PhD completion. Sufficient data, sufficient background research, and sufficient results were all relative. I now needed to convince the new jury that the plan (which half of them had helped me lay out mere months before) was still reasonable.

Even though I wasn't starting over from the beginning, I was starting new relationships, which could potentially affect my work. It wasn't just about mental preparedness, but at that point, I was vulnerable. It truly felt as if everything was becoming bigger than me. I realize this was one of the driving factors for me to see a therapist. I could no longer process everything that was happening around me on my own. Seeking the help that I needed, changed my trajectory and helped me return to the path I had veered off. Before long, I was once again ready to fight my way to the finish.

Finding committee members felt like déjà vu. But this time around, I knew exactly how to strategize. I was able to add one professor in particular who I admired. I had taken several of his classes, and he added a different dimension than what I previously had on my committee—specifically within the computing elements of my research. I believed he would be able to see the bigger picture of where my research would go.

The rest of the semester was spent figuring out my new normal and getting prepared for my first technical conference. I was debating whether I should go. It was bittersweet, because I had spoken about these moments with my past advisor so many times. I felt as if he was being cheated out of the opportunity to witness one of my milestones, but it was always important to him that the train kept going. I pressed on in his honor.

THE BIG GIRL MOMENT

Walking into the conference hall felt surreal and almost intimidating. It was hard to imagine that so many different individuals had similar ideas. We are all convinced that our research will break barriers; when we are surrounded by so many brilliant minds, there will be discussions that will cultivate even better ideas. It was hard for me to grasp that somewhere in this sea of hundreds, there was a handful of minds who were planning to attend my presentation and get a glimpse of my contributions to the field.

I had no right to experience imposter syndrome, because I did the work—yet, I couldn't shake it. Every individual spoke with such confidence, privilege, and belonging. There even seemed to be a sense of community based on the gender disparity alone. Though I was one out of a handful of Black women I had seen, I had to put my feelings aside and show my peers that my presence wasn't a fluke.

It was time to show that I knew my shit, and unsure stares weren't going to change that. Like some people, I have a fear of public speaking. When it came to my research, it was more than a fear—it was a phobia. What if someone asked me a question I didn't know the answer to? What would that say about the quality of my research?

The stress of my approaching presentation turned into stomach cramps—a sure sign that none of this was worth it. However, the research expert in me knew that conferences were another avenue for growth, and without growth, there was no real success. As I stood at the front of the room, I realized that this was the most people I had ever presented to. My terror turned into exhilaration as I quickly found my stride.

I realized that I had allowed negative thoughts to take away from how huge this was for my academic journey. Pushing through meant registering for my second conference in the spring. Next time around, I would be sure to show up with even more confidence and belonging.

THE REGROUP

By the time spring rolled around, I knew I had to regroup. I wished I could hit reset on the past six months. We always take for granted the second chances that we are given, but I have been told that there are no real second chances—only new paths. I was embarking on the new phase of my journey, which required I take the classes I had put off the semester before. It reminded me of my second year, only this time, I knew exactly where I was going. I was entering my semester of classes with the renewed confidence I lost earlier that year. No longer was I ashamed to ask questions while I sat in the front of the class, or care about how stupid I may have sounded. Things were different. My final years were about survival more than anything else, and it was a solitary road without my past advisor.

I spent the rest of the semester re-planning with my new advisor. The norm for my PhD program (and most programs) is that you publish three or four technical research papers and use those as your dissertation. Somewhere along the way, it all got lost in the shuffle. I only had three semesters left and no real artifacts to show. I submitted my first paper the year before, which was rejected; after the events of the fall, it was no longer worth it to try again. Do I regret it? At times. Even though I felt as if no one was there to push me, there was. There was me. But I had been so busy focusing on my despair that I let it feel impossible to rise above it.

My other option was to write a full dissertation from front to back, and use all of my research in it. Academic society made it seem like you were more respected as a PhD if you had papers under your belt. It was, quite literally, publish or perish. Society and their stigmas, I guess. But why was my accomplishment as a non-published PhD any less valid than anyone else's? Kudos to my new advisor for constantly reminding me of that, and for reminding me that my dissertation was going to speak for itself.

To be honest, my abilities have always leaned more towards math, not English. The thought of writing a two hundred-page document stressed me the hell out. If I chose the dissertation route, I had to make sure it was of great quality and quantity. Thinking about how I was going to culminate my remaining time at graduate school made it all real. However, this was the beginning of my transition towards greener pastures over in post-grad life. Although I still had one summer and an entire academic year to go, knowing that the exit strategy was in the works was enough to get me ready for the final act.

It was also time for me to plan for the post-graduate transition. Traditionally, PhD recipients going into academia get a post-doctoral fellowship, and then eventually become professors or researchers. It always seemed taboo for those with a PhD to go into industry; they're sometimes called sell-outs. If you are reading this and think that isn't true, I am giving you the ultimate side eye—we both know better. I must admit that strides are being made to ensure everyone feels equally encouraged and confident when it comes to their future choices.

Making sure I had a choice once I graduated was all that mattered to me, and thankfully, I had started to lay the groundwork early. It was more than a year from my graduation date when I started interviewing. Some may perceive this as early, but I was still interviewing well into my fifth year. I was only able to finalize a position five months before my graduation. I was also finally able to attend a career fair where I gave out countless copies of my resume. A PhD helps you become an expert, but also makes you become so streamlined that companies put you in a box for that specific subject.

Some students welcome and relish the opportunity to continue working on the topics they have been working on for the past five to seven years. For others (like me), they need to try something new, despite how difficult it may be. I didn't realize how much I lost myself in graduate school, which often made me feel like I no longer knew what I wanted to do. I knew what I didn't enjoy: I didn't enjoy the hours spent babysitting simulations while doing trial and error. Believe me, sometimes knowing what you don't want is just as important as knowing what you do. I wasn't sure where I fit in. On one hand, the opportunities presented to me were so specific to my research that the transition would be easy. On the other hand, I wasn't sure where I saw myself.

There were so many factors to consider, which made matters even more complicated. I just needed the right opportunity to wake up the dormant parts of me that had been on autopilot. After speaking to over a dozen companies, I found my match.

SUMMER FINALE

Being displaced from the lab made everything official. It had taken me such a long time to find an identity in that space. Thankfully, it would eventually grow to be a place where I finally felt like I belonged. It was difficult for me to come to terms with the fact that we were still dispensable. The space was no longer ours; it was time to clear it out for a new professor to occupy. The move also reminded me that there was no fallback plan. If this didn't work, I literally had nowhere to go. I had to push through, but what did "push through" mean? It meant using the last summer filled with empty days and full-time undergraduate students. It meant taking advantage of the fact that there were no imposed deadlines (except for the obvious one of graduating).

It was time to start from the beginning and explore the very first question asked about my research. I wanted to make sure that I didn't just have the answer to every question, but that I had the proof in the answers I provided. I was always told to dig deeper, whether it be in my literature research or questions I was asking myself after experiments. To me, that was just inconvenient; I already knew the answers. But with time, I realized I had to accept the responsibility of being a professional in my field. I had to be my biggest challenger, and my own devil's advocate.

Did it take more time? More than I would have liked, but it meant that I was covering all my bases. I had also promised myself that this would be my last summer in the program. And, as if the heavens heard my prayers, it was.

YEAR FOUR LESSONS

ALWAYS LISTEN

As my grandmother would say, "You have two ears and one mouth for a reason." This point is especially important when emotions are running high. The last thing you want to do is to make decisions based on your emotions, or say something before you've had time to think. Once you have all the facts, take the time to strategize. It is hard for us to make unbiased decisions when it comes to making decisions about ourselves, but you want to make sure that outside opinions and your own biases don't skew what should be your destined path forward.

DON'T SETTLE

There is a fine line between listening and settling. Even when it comes to listening to our own voice, we tend to not give ourselves the extra push we require. In the end, we unknowingly settle for less than we deserve. When you are confident in what you want (not an easy feat, but always worth it), you always trust yourself first! Starting over wasn't an option for me. I knew I wasn't going to settle for something that required me to find a new topic and possibly extend my time or research.

NEVER TOO EARLY TO JOB HUNT

There were 455 days left before graduation when I started laying the groundwork for my after-graduation job. I made continuous efforts to attend conferences, summits, and symposiums in my field. For every person I met with an interesting role, I followed up with a simple email thanking them for the opportunity to connect. Once graduation neared, I reconnected by first reminding contacts of where we had met. Then, I informed them of my impending graduation and asked to discuss any opportunities. At first, the timeline may seem too far out—but between follow-ups, letting people know that you are ready to apply for jobs, and the months of interviews, graduation will be here before you know it. Believe me, the only thing better than crossing the stage is knowing that you are crossing with a job secured.

One of graduate students' biggest stressors about job applications is not knowing whether we will be done on time. Of course, the definition of "done" is fluid, depending on your program and advisor, but you can use a job offer to help you accelerate where things may be dragging. If a job really wants you, they will wait for you (within reason). Always keep your advisor in the loop and let your them know you are planning to apply for jobs. This way, you have an expected timeline. Just remember that even when you think it is too early to look for a job, it is never too early to network.

FAMI-LAB AFFAIR

Your lab (or your group—whoever you work with under your professor), is your family, whether you like it or not. Even though I had found a tribe I could lean on, they weren't prepared to deal with something like the passing of my advisor. While they did their very best to console me, they had no idea how I felt about the loss and what it meant for me on multiple levels. The bonds you have with your lab mates and colleagues who work for the same advisor as you, are important. They become a different type of family. You can also leverage them to deal with your advisor or other lab/class related issues.

MENTAL HEALTH

Black women are always seen as strong. So, when everyone comes to us to solve the world's problems, who can we turn to when we're in turmoil? Even if we could seek out help, how could we? Would that not make us look weak?

The truth is, I don't know where I would have been if I didn't listen to my body and give my mental health the attention that it needed. Despite enduring something traumatic, I was quick to shake it off because I was afraid of how I would be perceived. Breaking down was the reminder that my well-being it isn't a game.

Letting my guard down and opening up to a therapist was one of the best decisions I made. It allowed me to take a moment to breathe and clearly think about the decisions I needed to make with someone who was qualified to listen and offer advice. Sometimes it wasn't even about a decision; it was about being in a safe place where I could let my frustrations out. If I hadn't gone through everything I did, I never would have known that therapy was easily accessible to me as a graduate student. I recommend using the therapy resources at your own institutions. Instead of waiting for tragedy to strike, do regular check-ins. We often think that therapy is only needed when we're at rock bottom. But you'll be surprised how much easier it is to bounce back when you have the right tools.

Never be ashamed to take the necessary steps for you. Know that it takes more strength to admit when something is wrong, and it takes even more strength to seek help. When I really needed an outlet, I would journal exactly what I was feeling. I often wondered if anyone knew what mental struggles and burdens were like for a Black woman in a white, male-dominated world. On one occasion, I wrote this as a release:

Mental Reality

I push, I toil, I heave, I try.
My will so strong, but still no rise.
A burden to carry, a burden to face.
Tasked as the token to represent with grace.
Being a token isn't a good thing. Terrible, matter of fact.

It shows system failures and the "diversity" we lack.
"Good for you," they say. "Keep going to the top."
But what's the point if there's no opportunity for others to follow up?
"I'm not racist, I support your cause," they say.
But what have you done to help as the moments keep

drifting away?
Mentally, I feel drained.
Every day I fight to remain "sane."
But what does sane really mean,
If every day I am waking up to trauma and
responsibility?
An environment that waters my sadness, discriminates
against my depression.
There's an invisible "no help wanted" sign. Since help is
viewed as a transgression,
As individuals we just want to do right.
But as a Black woman, that's just one of the battles we
must fight.
Doing right for me isn't silence—doing right is a
needed action,
Ensuring my voice is heard, despite anyone else's
reaction.

END OF CHAPTER WORKSHOP

What have I accomplished this year?

_____

_____

_____

_____

_____

_____

_____

_____

_____

What are some key things I would like to accomplish? Does this include conferences, journals, or networking events?

_____

_____

_____

_____

_____

_____

_____

_____

_____

What are some other listening exercises I can put into practice? (e.g. pause, think, repeat, answer)

_____

_____

_____

_____

_____

_____

_____

_____

_____

What are two things I can do to focus on my mental well-being?

_____

_____

_____

_____

_____

_____

_____

_____

_____

When I was told to dig deeper in my research, I started asking myself the Five Whys. I asked myself "why" until I had an explanation. Sometimes it took me three whys; other times, I needed to ask all five. One of the first times I did the Five Whys was during a failed experiment. This exercise helped me find the root cause of the failures, and eventually helped alleviate some of my frustrations.

What are my Five Whys?

_____

_____

_____

_____

_____

_____

_____

_____

_____

_____

YEAR FIVE

"Don't let anyone rob you of your imagination, your creativity, or your curiosity. It's your place in the world; it's your life. Go on and do all you can with it, and make it the life you want to live."

– Mae Jemison

THE TUNNEL VISION

It was finally time to get to writing. When I think of words to describe this process, all that comes to mind are grunts, sighs, and different tones of "ugh." If you have never had to write a personal statement or proposal, then you are in luck! A dissertation is nothing like those things. The dissertation was about putting all the extensive research and experiments I had done into one multi-chapter document that told my research story. Pressure came from a number of places. It came from knowing that this would be my legacy, and that anything I wrote would be referenced in the future. It came from self-doubt and wondering—even in the final hours of my graduate career—if my topic was novel enough.

When I think back on my fifth year in graduate school, I only seem to remember writing. Quite honestly, if you are going to get through your final year, you must have tunnel vision. It is as if you are in an exclusive relationship with school. I know this goes against some of my earlier points about balancing life, but there is no other way to describe it. This is where the sacrifices begin to pay off, but also when you are the most vulnerable.

Needless to say, I had felt like a fraud more than

ever. I suddenly felt like maybe I hadn't done enough in the past five years, and at every step, I thought my dissertation could have been better. Every decision, experiment, class, and article centered around this final document. It would basically prove if what I had to say was good enough to go beyond the graduate school walls. I wish I could say there was a plan that I was able to follow, or a chart that got me through, but there wasn't. Dissertating is truly dependent on the topic, the person doing it, and their advisor. There is no standardized approach, but I was able to give myself a head start by sketching out what my document would look like in terms of chapters and general topics.

Whether you have to write a 300-page dissertation or a long research paper, you need a beginning, middle, and end: where you came from, how you got there, and where you are headed next. While there isn't a how-to chart on how to get started, even having a simple approach will help. Think of it as the guard rails. Guard rails keep you safely within boundaries and prevent you from being deterred.

Between the multiple weekends of sitting well beyond eleven o'clock at night to get pages completed and repeating experiments to verify the results, my days and weekends were no longer differentiated. During this time, weekends didn't exist. The well-intended "it will pay off" was no longer comforting to me.

It's not just about being unable to attend social gatherings. I felt as if I was a prisoner of my work. Pursuing my degree was supposed to give me my independence, yet it felt as if I was trapped by it. Even *I* grew tired of hearing myself say, "I can't do anything this weekend." I knew I needed a well- deserved break, but I also couldn't get out of my own head and the fact that the stakes were extremely high. I couldn't nonchalantly ask about the worst that could happen, because the response was always the same. The worst that could happen is that I could fail, and for me, that was a gamble I wasn't ready to take.

Having your world and the way you live essentially centered around a single source is never a good thing. It's especially not worth it to have it centered around what you deem as success. Looking back now I realize that, but in the moment, it was a completely different story. The mounting pressures for minority graduate students is one of the major cycles that is difficult to break. It isn't feasible to excel the way you need to while thinking about all the people you are doing it for. That was the first thing I had to let go.

The second reason why writing a dissertation or graduating can't be the center of your life is because life happens, and sometimes you do fail. I have failed, and I know of people who have also failed at this point. But does that mean they weren't successful? For me to say that they failed would mean that there was no success beyond failure. But there was. If someone had told me that the world doesn't end if things don't go as planned, I would have still worked just as hard as I did—just not to the point where I thought my future plans for life would be ruined.

THE RELATIONSHIP STRAIN

Choosing my writing over socializing wasn't even the worst of it. When I said everything was centered over this one goal, I meant it. Because of my tunnel vision, many of my friendships suffered, and a couple of them became strained. Some relationships need constant stimulation, while others are on a sound enough foundation that they could withstand the biggest jolt. It is one thing to go down a different path—friends take different paths all the time—but when you are on a path that is also physically removed from your ties, challenges arise.

When your friends are free at night to chat or have a free weekend to go out, you aren't. Even when your friends decide to take a trip, you must consider the preplanning involved. It's not that you don't want to be there to share those moments; it's that you literally can't. I cried so many times when I missed amazing moments in my loved ones' lives, especially those who had known me before I started the graduate school journey. I missed birthdays, weddings, and children being born. It is a shitty feeling, to put it bluntly, and it's added to the fact that eventually people are going to stop asking you to join them altogether. Even though friends do their best to understand, you still hear and see the disappointment, and they have every right to feel that way.

The truth is they are trying to understand, but they don't. They know what you have sacrificed, but they still don't fully grasp how deep that sacrifice goes, and how the burden of not being around affects you. You are like an outsider looking into a circle that you no longer fit into.

Every one of my relationships was tested at one point or another, but the worst time was during my final year. During that time, nothing else seemed to matter. Failing wasn't an option. I had compromised over and over again, and there was no way that I had gone through all of that just to not finish. In my head, my friends were just going to have to understand. Was it fair to them? Definitely not. But it's real life, and you are probably nodding your head because you know exactly what I mean. I think it all came to a head when I was hundreds of miles away and one of my best friends passed away.

I wasn't just affected by her absence; I was affected by the fact that I had gotten buried by the work of research and the endless nights of experiments that I never found the time to check-in as often as I should have. She was the one who knew I needed a break before I did, and mobilized the friend brigade to sponsor me a trip to ensure that I didn't miss another celebration. That is the type of friend we all need. The ones who truly know you and can see you crumbling before you feel it. I realized I needed to start mending these relationships, because as crazy and burdensome my current experience was, it was also temporary.

So how is a strained friendship fixed? For me, I had to be purposeful. Even though I had amazing friends who understood, I also didn't want them to feel as if I took them for granted. I never wanted them to feel as if I didn't make time to even send a text. When my friend passed away, it really affected my future interaction with those close to me. It still does, and I am still learning to be firm when it comes to being intentional about checking in.

THE CAREER PATH

The reality is that no matter how much work you have to get done in your final year, it's doubled thanks to the mere fact that you are also adulting. There is a sense of relief mixed with fear because you are so overwhelmed that you actually made it to the end. I remember becoming emotional every time I reflected on the fact that I was almost there. A true emotional roller coaster, but I digress. The fear comes because, if you are like me, you haven't thought about what life is going to be like beyond school. Even though I knew that being on the lighter side of the publishing front didn't define my future and didn't take away from any future accolades I would receive, I still felt limited. I felt as if I didn't deserve to be a true academic.

Granted, academia was not my plan (although I would consider being an adjunct professor later on), it is always nice to have options. I started thinking about industry jobs and how I was going to transition from my current academic comfort zone to something very different. I was a true blank slate, with no prior internship experience.

I had completed all the steps in my previous year: research companies, go to conferences, network, land job interviews, and commit. But I was still hesitant. I felt as if I couldn't commit to a company when I had an entire dissertation to write. I barely knew when (or if) I was going to finish. I hoped for summer, but as you have probably experienced, there is no time stamp. This isn't a good enough reason to delay planning for your future, though. While I was looking for a job, I was also looking for a culture that best fit my plans for the future. This meant that the companies were on the interview bench as well. I needed to know where they saw a place for me, especially because my research was so specific.

I put so much pressure on myself about finding the right job that I forgot life is all about change, and a career is full of rotations. During graduate school, we are so bogged down by that one topic that we forget what it is like to shift gears. I had given myself a deadline to be finished, but I also was committed to something external. It was the pull I needed to make sure the deal was sealed. Companies understand that unexpected things happen, and that you may need to extend a few weeks. But I didn't want that. I was ready.

Of course, I couldn't just get up and decide that it was time to land a job and check it off the list. I still had the other half of my research partnership to consider. Before I started looking for a job, I discussed with my advisor my plan to start searching and see what opportunities were out there. Once the job offer came in, I told him of the expected start date and negotiated a reasonable timeline. You never want to go rogue. Always make sure you can get the positive support needed; even in the end, it's extremely vital. Once we were on the same page (or at least within the same chapter), I still had one job that was even more important than the one I was looking for: I had to finish my dissertation.

THE FINAL EXAM

I had never written so many pages of anything in my life. Chapters were by page dozens, and my references needed an entire chapter on their own. I thought the writing would never end until one day over the winter break, there I was, rounding out the conclusion. I couldn't believe that I had written over 180 pages. It is one accomplishment that still blows my mind. It wasn't as easy as typing the final period and calling it finished; I still had a revision phase to get through, but at least the heavy lifting was over. I also couldn't celebrate just yet—I still had to prepare for my dissertation defense in the middle of January. The dissertation defense was my swan song. Its purpose was to defend everything I had written in the dissertation.

There was still the matter of building the entire presentation while incorporating the feedback I received from my committee members. I also had to prepare for my mother's arrival, since she decided to make it an extra special defense by flying in from Trinidad. The plan was to have her arrive a few days before my defense, and then I would return with her for an extended vacation. How did that plan go? Well, if you have been paying attention, then you know by now that nothing ever went as planned.

The day before her arrival, we had one of the biggest winter storms on the East Coast. In between defense prep and edits, I tried to get her on any flight that would get her as close to upstate New York as possible. After three days (and two days before my defense), I realized she would not be able to get to me that easily. With only one last option to explore, I prayed it would work. It wasn't ideal, but it was going to have to do. Two days before my defense, she finally got a flight that would take her to an airport three and a half hours away. Before I could give it a second thought, I was already in my car to get her.

Despite the hassle, her company was exactly what I needed. I spent the days before sitting on pins and needles, not knowing that she was the comfort I needed. I practiced so many times with my different social groups, including my lab mates and my tribe, yet my stomach remained in constant knots. I could barely eat, and I didn't even really want to speak. Any questions my mother asked me while we were at dinner the night before were met with curt responses. I felt as if I needed to save my brain's energy for the next day's questions. Also, I don't know who came up with the saying "get a good night's rest," especially for a big event. I've barely slept the night before any big event. It was no different this time around, as I was restless the entire night and up before the alarm the next morning.

The ride to campus was quiet, and the walk from

the car was even more silent. Once I set up the room with a few goodies, there was nothing more to do but sit and wait. The department had sent out an announcement of my defense, so I had no idea what or who to expect. I was relieved when I saw familiar faces filing into the room—my tribe, lab mates, my students, and others from around campus. Once everyone was settled, my advisor set the stage and said this was the biggest crowd he had seen at a defense. Not only did that comment remind me that I had developed a much bigger support system throughout the years than I realized, but it gave me the validation that all these people were here to witness my expertise.

Once I got over the initial nervous energy I had from presenting in front of such a big crowd, the presentation pretty much went smoothly. There was a feeling of pride that came over me while I talked about the path I had taken to get to this point. This was my work. I did this. Of course, there were the expected challenging questions from the committee during the presentation, giving me the opportunity to justify every step and even missteps I may have taken during my research. As I exhaled in relief after the final public forum question was answered, the beaming faces staring back at me said it all: I killed it!

The real interrogation would happen after the public forum, during the closed session. After the presentation was complete and all the attendees had gone, we began what would be an additional hour of discussion. We addressed red flags, as well as what the final dissertation timeline would look like. This part is all about compromise and ensuring that you give yourself enough time to complete any outstanding tasks while not taking on anything new.

As soon as the agreement was reached, my committee signed what was probably the most important piece of paper I had held over the past five years. The ink was barely dry before I ran out screaming to my mother, who had sat patiently for an hour outside the room waiting. At this point, I was truly relieved. No matter what happened, I had fulfilled my requirements. My final dissertation was really just a formality.

I must have done at least ten iterations over the following four months before every committee member agreed that the final submission was ready. During this time, I wanted to make sure I found a few reliable people, other than my committee, who were willing to review my dissertation. It's not an easy ask when you are looking for someone to read over 180 pages of work. Make sure you have at least one person in your network who can review any section that you may need a second opinion on before you submit. For me, those people were my undergraduate mentor—and my father, who read at least three of my iterations.

Many students finally get through the struggle of writing and defending their dissertation, and still feel trapped. I have witnessed it and I prayed that I wouldn't fall prey to it. Luckily for me, it was a clean transition; I only had a couple months to pack up my apartment and move across the country to start my new job. It's important to find the balance between adding value to an already out-of-this-world achievement and being free labor (especially when the projects aren't even related to your work). This goes for any discipline. Make sure that you have an exit strategy once you defend and are ready to submit your final requirements. There is always going to be a situation when, even after the defense is completed and the dissertation is done, you'll need to do a little extra work. Maybe it's a grant that needs to get done, or two brand new journals to be written out of the blue. Know what you are committing to, and ensure you get credit.

THE COMMENCEMENT

The five years had felt excruciatingly long—yet here I was, one week before graduation, scrambling to make what would be the perfect weekend for myself and all my guests. Caribbean families tend to roll deep for all celebrations, because an accomplishment for one is an accomplishment for all of us. I had at least thirty-five loved ones coming to show their support that weekend. The ceremonies had a ticket cap limit of three tickets. Despite the restriction, I knew they'd find a way to be in my corner, cheering me on the loudest. I mean, I did say thirty-five people, right?

People claim to understand exactly how epic the weekend was going to be, but no one really knew the significance except for others who had experienced it. I had spent several years in the backwoods of New York away from family and friends. This wasn't just my graduation; this was my coming out. I was also celebrating my transition from student life, all-nighters, and the permanency of single life that the small town had so graciously bestowed upon me.

The celebration was held over the course of two days, due to the multiple ceremonies required by the school. I had been extra meticulous in planning the weekend with activities. At some point, the event began to sound like a wedding, minus the groom. I had two sides of the family coming in from around the country and Trinidad. The weather called for a nice and sunny weekend, but we were prepared for overwhelming heat on the Saturday. After all, it had been thirty years since it rained in this college town on graduation weekend.

On the first day we had a wine tour event inclusive of family and friends. The wine tour went smoother than expected, considering there was easily twenty of us. This, however, wasn't the day's big challenge. They had warned about extreme heat conditions, but we weren't warned about the suffocating heat that would result from non-air-conditioned indoor facilities. After a fun day of wine tasting, we arrived at the weekend's first graduation ceremony, which was taking place at the indoor track. In no world does the combination of alcohol followed by broiler conditions fair well. But the fact that my family was still the loudest cheering section (according to the Dean) reminded me that this wasn't just a milestone in my journey, but also in theirs.

Lining up for the official graduation procession the following day and processing from the middle of the campus grounds to the stadium, felt surreal.

Everything I had worked for culminated to this moment. With my "Trini" flag in hand, I was ready to wave to all the passersby who had lined the campus streets. It is a different kind of feeling, having complete strangers congratulate you. I felt like I could burst from joy with every step I took. To see my other co-graduates sit on the open field, as well as those in the stands, made what happened next almost forgettable. Almost. The second day of ceremonies was much cooler than the day before. As a matter of fact, it was so cool that the perfect record of no rain in thirty years they had boasted about was suddenly broken. We didn't have just a drizzle; we had a full-blown thunderstorm. As we ran out of the stadium to our various departments for the individual ceremonies, I prayed that it would stop, even just for a moment, so everyone could enjoy what was happening. After all, it was historic.

By the time I got down to my department, which held their graduation in a tent, the rain had stopped—but I was drenched. My graduation gown felt ten pounds heavier and after how long I waited for this moment, I wasn't about to take it off. For the third and final ceremony, I once again had my section of supporters, which was way past the three-person limit. As expected, they wanted everyone to know what they were there for, so they sat in the front rows as the PhD graduates sat on the stage. There they were, able to see the young Black girl from the island who blossomed into an ivy league graduate woman sitting on the stage. The only one. For them to be able to witness the moment when I walked to the front of the stage to be hooded made it all worth it. I was even happier knowing that the PhD graduates went first, especially when the thunderstorms resumed just as the undergraduate students were crossing the stage (and they were only on the letter *B*).

The ceremony represented the complexity of my journey to get there. There were storms that threatened my future, and beautiful moments of sunshine that amplified my highs. It felt rewarding to see my tribes, new and old, come together and celebrate the fact that it had all worked out, just as it was supposed to.

WHAT'S NEXT?

Throughout the past five years of graduate school, I have said more times than necessary that I couldn't wait for "real life" to begin. What I didn't realize is that I had made the best of my time without even trying—from the people I met to the places I had traveled to and all my firsts.

I went from not knowing if I would ever graduate with a degree to sitting on a plane, headed to a completely different coast for the next phase of my life. My heart raced, excited for what was sure to be an unforgettable five years to come.

As a student, feelings of joy and relief represent parts of your life at different steps of your journey. But as a student of color – a Black student, these same feelings are elevated by the notion that you are representing not just the people who look like you, but your family—especially as a first or second-generation college student. No matter what they are, your feelings are valid and should always be celebrated.

YEAR FIVE LESSONS

FORGIVING POSSE

It's not just about finding a tribe while you are in school—you have to make sure the people who have always been with you are forgiving friends, forgiving partners, and even forgiving family members. The last thing you need during one of the toughest times in your life is someone making you feel guilty or calling you out for being a terrible human being. You are not perfect, and forgiving people know this. Once the dust has settled, they may be a little salty, but they will also be right by your side to continue on with you.

My Tribe…
I look at the smiling faces,
Your love shown from different places,
Realizing that we are all alone together,
Showing that we are stronger than the majority because we are drawn to one another.
My confidence was lost but now it is found
And I'm ready to be that little Black girl they gave a chance,
Making my own damn self proud.
Finding that inner strength; a blessing in disguise.
Without my Lord and Savior, I could not survive.
Without you, my comrades, my friends, my day ones, and my boos,
I would have never been able to show Cornell exactly what strong Black women do.

EXIT STRATEGY

What's an exit strategy? Good ol' Wikipedia says: "An exit strategy is a means of leaving one's current situation...after a predetermined objective has been achieved."

This definition sums it up perfectly. The objective is to get that degree, submit all requirements, and leave! We have to think about the follow-up once the objective has been achieved. If there is a strategy in play, then it's easy to take the next steps.

Here are some helpful questions to ask yourself:

Do I want to work in industry or academia?

_____

_____

_____

_____

_____

_____

_____

_____

_____

_____

_____

Do I think I have a year or less left before graduation?

_____

_____

_____

_____

_____

_____

_____

Does my advisor agree that I have a year or less left before graduation?

_____

_____

_____

_____

_____

_____

What are the requirements for me to graduate?

_____

_____

_____

_____

_____

_____

What are the expectations of my advisor for me to graduate?

_____

_____

_____

_____

_____

_____

Will it be a clean transition? Am I expected to stay a semester or summer beyond?

_____

_____

_____

_____

_____

_____

Do I have an idea of where I want to work?

_____

_____

_____

_____

_____

_____

Is my resume updated? What do I still need to add?

_____

_____

_____

_____

_____

_____

_____

Do I have any career fair/interview interactions planned?

_____

_____

_____

_____

_____

_____

_____

DON'T SECOND GUESS YOUR CHOICES

Every choice you make has a ripple effect. Whether it is a small splash or a tidal wave, you have to take everything into consideration. Does that mean you have to figure out which choice is the right one at the beginning of the year? No. Choices can change, and nothing is permanent. It is just a little harder to believe because you have studied the same topic and worked towards one goal for several years. But beyond school, goals change, and you can be anything you choose to be. You don't have to be the person you thought you would be in school. I made the choice to go into industry and I also made the choice (although it can be argued that it was influenced by circumstances), to write a full dissertation instead of fully publishing. With these choices, I had to weigh the options and the possible consequences that each of them would have. But once I made the choice, I needed to stay grounded and truly experience what lay ahead of me, rather than look back at what might have been.

QUICK REFLECTION

1. My first year was filled with exploration: exploration of self, exploration of research, and exploration of partnership.

   It was more than just a new chapter in my life; it was a path to self-discovery. On the path to self-discovery, I encountered early failures in classes and PhD qualifying exam prep. I had to realize that there was a lot more headed my way. If you really want to test your strength, go to graduate school. I had to discover what my true interests were, so that I didn't get lost in the first-year shuffle.

   During this year, I explored different research topics to help me find my niche and understand what it meant to be a researcher. I needed to find a research topic that didn't make my frustration outweigh my fascination. The most important exploration came in finding an advisor who would be my partner throughout graduate school. After having numerous informal interviews with different professors, I still consider the choice of advisor to be one of the most important decisions I have made.

2. Preparing for my PhD qualifying exam was the theme of my second year's fall semester. I tried to leverage the required classes to gain knowledge on what might be coming on the exam. Fortunately, during that time, I also found my tribe through a chance encounter with another Black woman attending one of my classes. She took me to the gatherings and gave me access to what I didn't realize was one of the missing pieces of my graduate school experience.

   The people we meet in graduate school are the beginning nodes to our professional network. Understanding how these relationships can be both supportive and productive is key. Thanks to them, I had people to lean on, especially as I began navigating the world of research and the responsibilities that came with having undergraduate researchers reporting to you.

3. With a little patience and time, I was able to find my rhythm. I had the teaching assistant schedule down, and I finally had my experiment schedule for my research. I also became the lead graduate student to a few undergraduate students, which

was daunting and made me question my leadership skills at times. I was in control and their failures were tied to mine, which meant it wasn't the time to be timid about my expectations.

I was halfway through my journey, which meant that Murphy's Law was very much still in effect. During that time, it was important to remember the "why" of graduate school.

4. Adversity comes in many forms, and my fourth year didn't fall short of any of them. After a devastating loss, picking up the pieces seemed impossible, but using what I had learned from previous challenges gave me the inner strength I needed.

Having a tribe to lean on while I decided on my new path is also what I needed. I was past the midway point now. I was also exposed to technical conferences, which I took full advantage of. The fact that I was one of a few Black women—or the only Black woman— in any room was unmistakeable, but fading into the background wasn't an option. I had to own my research, my facts, and what I was presenting. I became the expert in the room, which fueled me with confidence.

5. The finish line to-do list seemed to be the gift that kept on giving. From the continuous writing and revisions of my dissertation to ensuring I was ready for the job market, with endless interviews scattered in between, I wasn't just preparing to finish the race—it was the championship.

   The final year focused on my exit strategy and aligning it with my writing. I found it difficult to balance what I needed to accomplish for school and what I needed for the next phase of my life. In the end, I discovered it was all worth it.

EPILOGUE

I hope my collection of thoughts has shown you that while some are threatened by your Blackness, your success, and your impact, you have the ability to make it as a powerful Black individual. You will find those who will lift you up, become allies, and shower you with support. I pray that my journey gives you encouragement and helps you make your journey even better. Be proud and confident in your own likeness, even when others abuse it or don't see it.

Most of all, be loyal to YOU. It is easy to sell yourself short and let setbacks and obstacles get the best of you. Never forget who you are and who you would like yourself to be. Grow comfortable in your own skin and be brave, bold, and graceful. Remember: you are a warrior and you worked hard to be here. Get that degree, girl!

SPECIAL ACKNOWLEDGMENTS

I continue to believe that I am the living embodiment of God's purpose for my life. Therefore, my thanks go out to Him, first and foremost.

To my mother Jennifer—thank you for being my rock and for believing in this project, even when I put it down so many times throughout the years. Thank you to my father Stephenson, who reminded me to keep a record of everything. I'd say I did pretty well! It finally paid off. Thank you both for the little reminders along the way, and for being supportive as I took the risk of opening up to the world. To my siblings, thank you for being there as a part of my wonderful support system!

To my sis-cousins, Kenya and Tylisha—thank you for never letting me settle for mediocrity in times of doubt. You pushed and motivated me to complete my first draft and made sure that I kept going.

To my editor and friend, Melissa Murphy, with

every reading, you helped me find my voice and ably critiqued my manuscript. I also extend my gratitude to Adam Allred, who took my words years ago and helped shape what would be the beginning of this amazing journey. You helped lay the foundation.

Having an idea and writing your story is one thing, but having a team that believes in its value is another. Thank you to the Mynd Matters Publishing team for making sure my vision became a reality. A special thank you to my cover illustrator, Lauren Harris, who created beauty far beyond what my imagination could reach.

To my mentor, Akibi, one of my first readers—I am so grateful to you for sticking with me all these years, and for letting me be vulnerable when it came to sharing this project with you.

To my loving and supportive family and friends who have been the ultimate tribe throughout the years. Even from afar, you continue to keep me grounded. To my Trini posse, you have always showed out and been my biggest cheerleaders.

And where would I be without my Adelphi tribe? You make a girl feel loved and supported, always. To the tribe in this book, my graduate school family who got me through, I literally wouldn't be writing this if you weren't there to keep me sane. Though we've been through it all, some of my happiest memories have come from the time we spent together.

So many others have encouraged and supported me throughout this journey, and I express my deepest gratitude to the roles you continue to play in my life.

We hope you enjoyed *Hooded: A Black Girl's Guide to the Ph.D.* and will take a few minutes to leave a review. Writing a review helps an indie author more than you know!

To learn more, visit the author's website at www.MalikaGrayson.com.

Printed in the USA
CPSIA information can be obtained
at www.ICGtesting.com
LVHW041700051023
760086LV00058B/1384